THE
Archive Photographs
SERIES

SALISBURY

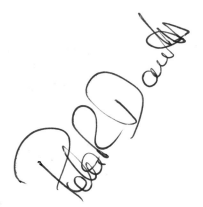

THE GIANT AND HOBNOB AT SALISBURY MUSEUM, 1898.

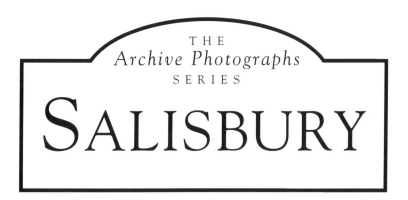

THE
Archive Photographs
SERIES

SALISBURY

Compiled by
Peter Daniels

CHALFORD

First published 1995
Copyright © Peter Daniels, 1995

The Chalford Publishing Company
St Mary's Mill, Chalford,
Stroud, Gloucestershire, GL6 8NX

ISBN 0 7524 0347 8

Typesetting and origination by
The Chalford Publishing Company
Printed in Great Britain by
Redwood Books, Trowbridge

A NOVELTY PICTURE POSTCARD OF SALISBURY CATHEDRAL, DATED 16 MARCH 1907.

Contents

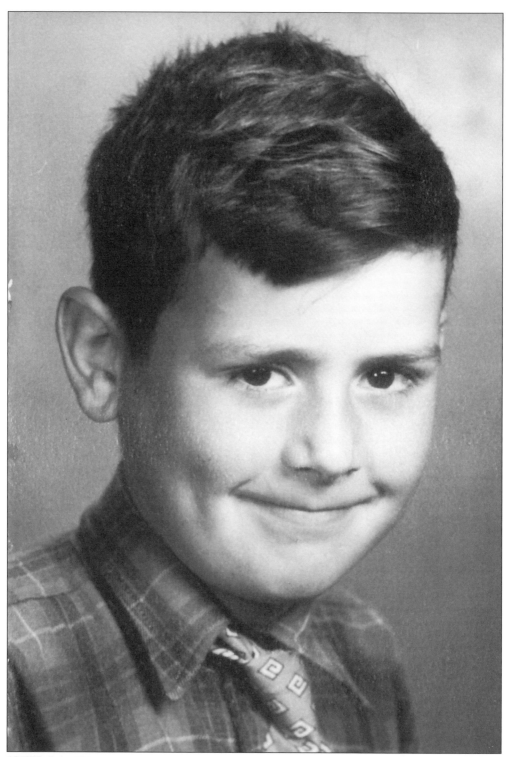

PETER DANIELS, AT THE AGE OF EIGHT. Dating from 31 May 1957, the photograph was taken at Saint Martin's Primary School in Saint Martin's Church Street.

Introduction

My interest in local history emerged in the mid-1970s, following a brief encounter with a new 35mm camera. I remember spending a day at the great Dorset steam fair, which was then held at Stoupaine Bushes, near Blandford. I returned home late in the afternoon, having taken more than a hundred pictures. There is no doubt that I took full advantage of all the photo opportunities that presented themselves on that particular occasion!

The prints of the road locomotives were brilliant, but I was even more pleased with the photographs I had produced of a few old lorries, cars and vans. With the desire to learn more I started to buy books on the subject and began to search for contemporary material. Among the items I sought were original photographs, postcards, business stationery and sales brochures. The hunt was very rewarding and I gathered together a great deal of information.

A year or two after starting my collection I acquired a small booklet from the late Jim Smith, who was proprietor of The Little Junk Shop at 73 Greencroft Street. It was a purchase that was to have a profound effect on my hobby. Written by Jeremy P. Farrant, the pamphlet was titled *Scout Motors of Salisbury, 1902-1921*. I was fascinated with the book and after reading it several times there were a number of questions that I wanted to ask, but I could find no one to answer them. Wanting to know more about the firm, I carried out a great deal of my own research. I learned a lot about the company and the vehicles they made. I also compiled lists of names of many of the first Scout car and commercial vehicle owners, who appear to have been mostly professional people, such as doctors, farmers and business men.

It was at this point in time that I realised my research had only just begun. There was so much more that could be done with the catalogue of names. There were so many questions that needed to be answered. For instance, what could be found out about the Revd William Page Roberts? It was all very well knowing that he had purchased a blue and yellow Scout limousine in February 1909 (registration number AM-1342), but I knew nothing else about him. I wanted to know what he looked like. I wanted to know where he lived. I simply wanted to learn more about him. Fortunately, the enquiries that I made in that direction were quite rewarding as I was able to find several photographs of him plus a few personal details. (He was installed as the Dean of Salisbury in 1907 and was succeeded in 1920. He lived in the Deanery, in the Cathedral Close, of which I now possess many old photographs.). My work is not always as successful as this, however. Sometimes the facts sought about a certain person, organisation, or event just cannot be found, even if the search was an especially thorough and extensive one. There is a great deal of research still to be done.

My first illustrated article was published in the *Salisbury Journal* in 1980. It was the first of many. Then, in 1987, I was fortunate to be offered a regular weekly slot in the *Salisbury Times*. It was an opportunity that could not be missed. The 'Puzzle Picture' series was introduced and it has been running ever since. Old photographs appeal to a wide audience, some of whom enjoy the feeling of nostalgia, while others are more interested in the historical aspects. Almost 400 pictures have appeared in the series thus far, all of which might otherwise never have been seen by the general public. It has been a great pleasure and a privilege to have met so many interesting people during the time that I have worked on the series. I have been sent a great many photographs, postcards, books and numerous other items of printed ephemera from all four corners of the earth. There is enough material available to keep me busy for many years to come.

This brings me neatly on to my latest project, *Salisbury*, in *the Archive Photographs series*. This volume differs from my previous books in so much that it includes sections of photographs that are dedicated to a number of specific events, all of which are appropriate to the city at this time. The pictures in Section 3, for instance, tell the story of The Guildhall, which is now 200 years old, and those in Section 5 show the Salisbury General Infirmary, which was recently closed. The photographs in Section 6 are dedicated to Salisbury at the time of the Second World War, which ended exactly fifty years ago. There are also selections of photographs that depict people and the commercial side of life. The pictures have been taken by numerous photographers, of whom some are anonymous, but those which appear on pages 47 to 72 were all produced by one individual, the late Austin Underwood. At the end of the book can be found a list of professional photographers who were working in the city from the 1850s to the 1960s. This information is very useful when one is estimating the date of a photograph that shows the name and/or address of the original photographer.

Peter R. Daniels
Netherhampton, October 1995

One
People

WORKING AT WATERLOO MILLS IN AROUND 1906. The individuals pictured here were employed by Henry Job Sutton, at the Steam Roller Flour Mills in Waterloo Gardens, Southampton Road. W. Lampard can be seen on the far left of the photograph and next to him is Edwin Beckley, then G. Shearing, G. Baker, Fred Smith and A. Musselwhite, who is on the extreme right. Mr Seywell is seated in the foreground.

THE RIGHT REVEREND JOHN WORDSWORTH, 1905, consecrated as the 93rd Bishop of
Salisbury on 28 October 1885. The eldest son of the Right Reverend Christopher Wordsworth,
87th Bishop of Lincoln, he was born at Headmaster's House, Harrow, on 21 September 1843.
He was educated at Ipswich Grammar School, Winchester, and New College, Oxford. He
resided at The Bishops Palace, The Close, Salisbury; Bishops Cottage, West Lulworth, Dorset;
and The Lollards' Tower, Lambeth, London S.E. Twice married, his first spouse was Susan
Esther (married 1870), daughter of Reverend H.O. Coxe, Bodley's Librarian, Oxford. She died
in 1894. Two years later he married Mary Anne Frances, daughter of Colonel R. Williams MP,
of Bridehead, Dorchester. The Bishop passed away at the Palace on Wednesday 16 August
1911. He was 68 years of age. His name is still frequently used in Salisbury as he was the founder
of Bishop Wordsworth's school. Established in Exeter Street over a hundred years ago, the
institution was originally known as The Higher Grade and Organised Science schools.

10

SALISBURY CITY FOOTBALL CLUB, 1908. Robbins, Stead, Meston, Hammond and Howshall can be seen in the back row, and pictured from left to right in row two are Musselwhite, Dowley, Metcalf and Jones. Yates, Burns, Cavendish and Candy appear in the front line.

THE ROYAL COUNTIES SHOW, 1934. The first event of its kind to be held in Salisbury since 1881, the show opened on 6 June. It took place in a field beside the Wilton Road, a few hundred yards beyond Skew Bridge. The picture shows the Duchess of York (now Queen Elizabeth the Queen Mother) presenting prizes in the juvenile class. Pictured here among the contestants is Daphne Whitehead (later Mrs Greville-Heygate), who proudly accepted a 'Highly Commended' certificate from the Duchess. She rode a friend's pony which was named Brown Sugar.

CROWDS OF SPECTATORS IN LIFEBOAT FIELD, 1907. Following a procession around the city streets, the Chapel Lifeboat (ON217) was launched from Lifeboat Field, which is on the south bank of the River Avon. Situated beside New Bridge Road, the field is now frequently used for car boot sales, and sadly it is all too often mistakenly called the Greyfisher Field. On this particular day £100 was collected and donated to the RNLI.

FORTY MEMBERS OF STAFF AT THE GAUMONT PALACE. Taken in the 1930s, the photograph shows the employees assembled at the main entrance to the cinema in The Canal. Pictured among the group is Irene Orchard (later Mrs Argent Parrish), Bill Drake, Nellie Dart and Fred Amps. At the time of this photograph the cinema was owned by Gaumont-British Picture Corporation Limited.

THE WHITEHEAD FAMILY, AT ROUGEMONT, LONDON ROAD, 1922. Arthur Whitehead (born 1860) can be seen in the centre of the picture. A solicitor by profession, during the 1880s he was in partnership with Edward Frederick Kelsey, at 32 Catherine Street. Subsequently he was to be found at 35 Canal, at the offices of Whitehead, Vizard, Ven and Lush. He was Mayor of Salisbury in 1892 and again in 1896. His sons Arthur junior (eldest) and Christopher are at the back of the group. Jo Hewsen is seated on the left with his son, Eric, on his lap. Jo married Dorothy Whitehead, who was Arthur's only daughter. The young boy sitting on the grass is Peter, the son of Arthur junior. On the right is Brian Whitehead and his son, Brian junior.

A VISIT FROM RICHARD TODD, THE FILM STAR, 1952. On Monday 9 August a crowd of more than 2,000 packed the Guildhall Square to see Mr Todd officially open the Salisbury Centenary Exhibition, 1852-1952, which was arranged in a large marquee in the Market Place. One of the more popular exhibits was to be seen on the *Salisbury and Winchester Journal* stand, where a printing press had been set up to produce a miniature souvenir version of the newspaper. On the front page was a report about the hundreds of teenage girls seeking the autograph of the actor who starred in the film *Robin Hood*, which had been shown at the Gaumont during the previous week. The photograph shows Mr Todd walking towards the marquee. His escort is Sergeant Cobden of the Salisbury City Police, and following on behind is Councillor 'P.J.' Southon and Mr W.J. Vizard.

Opposite: WINNERS OF THE SALISBURY INTER-HOUSE DARTS LEAGUE, 1950. Seated here in front of The Blackbird Inn in Churchfields Road are Tom Burden, Charlie Sedgwick, Charlie Dash, Harry Lear, Percy Cross and Archie Voce. With Percy Maple, Mick Hopgood, John Morgan and Harold Nelmes standing behind. The team also won the Salisbury Area Knock-out Cup in the Lamb Brewery League.

THE WEDDING OF AMELIA FLORENCE BLEW AND DOUGLAS JOHN BISS, 1910.
Taken at a time when wedding photography was a serious business, the picture shows the bride
and groom, the bridesmaids, Dorothy Balster, Winnie Blew, Daisy Blew and Marjorie Balster,
and the best man, Frank Gordon Biss, who was the groom's brother. They are pictured in the
garden of 15 Churchfields Road.

A SAINT BERNARD NAMED SOLOMON, c. 1950. Bred by Mr Gaunt at Cornagath Kennels in Ripley, Yorkshire, Solomon was the pride and joy of Dorothy and Michael Stefano, of Milford Street, Salisbury. He was just 10 months old when this photograph was taken. His diet included a pint of milk a day, plus daily doses of cod liver oil and extract of malt. At one time he weighed approximately 10 stones (63.5 kg). Although he suffered from heart trouble he lived until the late 1950s. The children who knew him loved him; the author was among them.

AT THE CO-OPERATIVE BAKERY IN ENDLESS STREET. Standing from left to right: Jack Strange, Douglas Chinn, Tom Broomsgrove, Fred Smith, Harold Strange, Sid Harwood and George Phillips. Seated is Ted Warren (confectionery manager) and Mr A. Darling (bread manager). The picture was taken before 1930.

HORACE CHARLES MESSER (1866-1936). Known as Charlie to his friends, Mr Messer left Ealing in 1889 and emigrated to Canada to practise photography. He remained there for six years. Then, in 1896, he came to Salisbury and took over the established photographic studio of John Arney and Son at 29 Castle Street. The business progressed well, and over a period of about twenty years Charlie produced thousands of quality photographs depicting the people, places and events of Salisbury. (His photographic postcards and enlargements are very much sought after by present day collectors.) In the late 1920s he returned to Ealing with his second wife, Lillian Pinner, and set up an electric light studio in Florence Terrace. This carte-de-visite portrait of him was produced in around 1891, at William Notman & Son's studio in Montreal.

LES PINNER ON HIS GRANDFATHER'S SHOULDERS, 1921. Les (aged five) is pictured here with George Thomas Pinner, in the garden of 112 Exeter Street. During the early 1900s George was employed as a foreman at Hardy & Son's aerated water manufactory at 31 Brown Street but was later dismissed for skylarking around with his men. He then went on to set up his own mineral water factory at the lower end of Brown Street. In addition to this he ran a haulage business and served the community as a special police constable. This photograph of him was entered for a competition in the *Weekly Dispatch* in 1921, but we do not know if it won any prizes.

Two
Commerce

A FODEN STEAM WAGON AT THE RAILWAY SIDINGS, 1920s. A crane can be seen lifting the furniture container off the back of the lorry before lowering it onto the platform of a railway wagon. Fred Smith was the driver of the Foden steam wagon. His brother-in-law, Walter Palmer, is pictured to the right. Their wives were sisters. Fred was married to Alice May and Walter was married to Pollyanna May.

THE CLOVELLY SCHOOL OF MUSIC, 1904. The school proprietress was Mrs Charlotte Bath, who can be seen standing on the pavement. Formerly at 3 Rampart Road, at the time of this photograph the school was to be found at 62 Rampart Road, which was also Mrs Bath's private residence. By 1911 the school had moved to 40 Harcourt Terrace. The house pictured here was later occupied by John Gray Percy, a dairyman. It was one of numerous dwellings that were demolished to make way for the Churchill Way relief road.

NICHOLAS BROTHERS HORSE-DRAWN DELIVERY VAN, 1911. The vehicle can be seen here at Victoria Park on the occasion of the RSPCA cart horse parade, which took place on Whit Monday. Nicholas Brothers' business premises were to be found at 44 Silver Street, 'Cafe Nicholas', and at 25-29 Wilton Road, which incorporated a bake house, a sub-post office and a grocery department. The firm had been established since 1840.

RED, WHITE AND BLUE FISH AND CHIP RESTAURANT, 1937. The business was started here at 51 Catherine Street by Oliver 'John' Reynolds and his wife Ethel, who moved to Salisbury from Burnham-on-Crouch, Essex in 1936. The photograph records the month of May 1937 and the occasion of King George VI's coronation. A colourful display of crowns, flags and ribbons can be seen in the shop window, in addition to the permanent signs which could usually be seen there, of which the following are examples: 'Snacks', 'Bed & Breakfast', 'Pot of Tea, 5d', 'Fish & Chips', 'Fresh Cut Sandwiches'. Another poster informs the passer-by that a family pet had gone missing. It reads, 'Lost, Siamese Cat'. Pictured here in front of the shop are Betty and Jim, who were not the only children in the family. Their sister, Josephine, can be seen in the photograph that is reproduced on page 42. Their father passed away in 1938. Ethel later opened a sweet shop at 79 Brown Street.

JOSEPH POWNEY'S SHOPS IN MINSTER STREET, 1905. Percy Harold Elliott can be seen standing in the doorway of number 9 Minster Street, on the extreme right of the photograph, which is now The Salisbury Studio. He left Powney's in 1912 and became proprietor of the Castle Street boat house and pleasure boats, following the death of his father, Alfred John Elliott. The shop in the foreground of the picture is number 7 Minster Street, which is now The Golden Curry (Indian restaurant). A selection of trousers is on display here in the price range 2s 11d to 3s 11d. Jackets are priced in the region of 6s 11d and waistcoats at 4s 6d. On the left of the picture, one can just see the gate and passage that leads to St Thomas's church.

Opposite: THE HEAD POST OFFICE IN THE CANAL, 1904. Situated at 21 The Canal since before 1857, the building was vacated in March 1907, which is when the present day main post office was opened in Castle Street. J. Sainsbury & Company took over the premises and for a number of years the Salisbury branch of their wholesale grocery business could be found here. A Marks and Spencer store occupies the site today.

SYDNEY ROBBINS' BAKERY AT 22 TRINITY STREET, 1911. Known as the Hygienic Steam Bakery, the business had been established half a century when this photograph was taken. These details appear in sign-writing on the back of the hand-cart that is depicted to the left. In addition to the bread and cakes that are on display in the shop window, there are numerous boxes of Fry's chocolates and jars of sweets to be seen. The Lacewing shop is here now.

MICHAEL AND DORIS AT SALISBURY MARKET, 1928. Michael Stefano (1904-1987) was known as the Banana King. He met Dorothy 'Doris' March at Frome, Somerset in around 1924, and soon afterwards they were married. They came to Salisbury in 1925 and started out in business selling cabbages that were supplied by Fred Andrews of Wishford Farm. They acquired their first lorry in 1928 (pictured above) and they were awarded a contract to ripen bananas for the Fyffes company. Their warehouse was to be found in Milford Street. In this photograph Doris is wearing a white coat. Michael stands near the cab of his Model-A Ford lorry. George Cave is on the extreme left and Sam Sawyer can be seen among the people on the right of the picture. Michael and Doris retired in 1975 and their son Don carried on the business until around 1987. One of their family pets was a very well-known and popular character, a photograph of whom appears on page 16.

Opposite: A SCOUT TAXI, MADE IN SALISBURY IN 1913. Louis Conio is sat behind the wheel of a 12-14hp blue tourer (AM-3030) that was manufactured at the Scout Motor Works in Churchfields Road, in April 1913. His employer, John Nash, can be seen in the front passenger seat. J. Nash & Sons of 82-84 Castle Street were already running a Scout car when this one was purchased. The previous model was a dark green landaulette (AM-2787) that was registered on 27 November 1912.

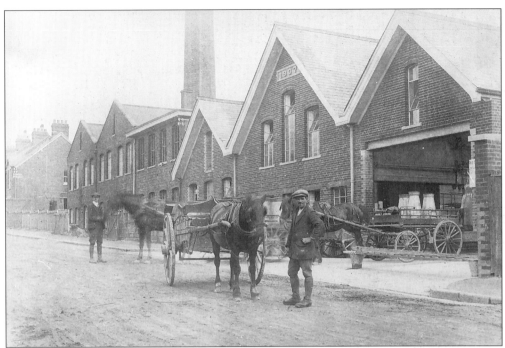

THE FUSSELL & COMPANY MILK FACTORY IN RUSSELL ROAD, 1915. The milk receiving bay can be seen on the extreme right of the picture, which is where the horse-drawn carts were unloaded. The churns of milk they carried had been produced on several local farms. A large slab of stone was built into the gable end of the factory showing the year that Messrs Wort and Way developed the area — 1907. The factory was demolished some years ago and numerous modern houses were built on the site. The 1907 stone was rescued and set into a brick wall on the edge of the estate, which is where it can still be seen today.

THE QUICK TURNOVER, 1936. Stanley 'Mick' Victor Gill and his wife Lilly moved to Salisbury from Shepherds Bush, London, just a short time before the creation of this picture. Their worldly possessions were transported here in Ford Model A lorry. Following a period of living in rented accommodation the couple purchased their own house in Queen's Road. Mick managed to secure his first pitch at Andover market some weeks before the inaugural appearance of The Quick Turnover fruit and vegetable stall in Salisbury. The original site was near the Singer Sewing Machine depot at 20 Oatmeal Row, but a short time later the firm was allocated a prime spot in the Guildhall Square. This is where 'Vic' Gill can still be seen on Tuesday and Saturday each week carrying on the very popular business set up by his father 60 years ago.

Three

Civic Pride

(The Council House,
Guildhall and Guildhall Square)

AN EDWARDIAN VIEW OF THE COUNCIL CHAMBER FROM QUEEN STREET. The original council house was built in 1573, roughly where the present day War Memorial is. On the occasion of the mayor-making banquet on 17 November 1780, a fire started in the Council House attic which virtually destroyed the building and left it unsafe. Seven years later Lord Radnor proposed to pay for a new chamber to be built. His offer was accepted and a foundation stone was laid on 14 October 1788. The new Council House was opened on 23 September 1795.

THE EARLIEST KNOWN PHOTOGRAPH OF THE COUNCIL CHAMBER, 1857. This remarkable photograph clearly shows a number of features that cannot be seen today. The western portico was carefully removed in 1889 and the columns were kept for repairing the northern portico (which was itself the result of improvements that were carried out in 1828). At the same time several new prison cells were installed on two levels of the building. Further internal alterations took place in 1896/97. The ornate wrought iron railings and arches that were to be found on the north and west boundaries of the council house can just be seen in this photograph. They were taken away sometime before 1885. One's attention is also drawn to the extreme right of the picture, which shows that the south-east corner of the Market Place remained undeveloped at this time. In around 1904, however, a large building was erected at the eastern end of Ox Row, the first occupiers being Thomas Bowden Bennett (wholesale haberdasher and general warehouseman) and Edward Montague Whaley (hosier).

Opposite: THE SEBASTOPOL CANNON, 1914. This relic was positioned on a plinth in the north-east corner of the Council House (see page 27). It was taken away in 1943 and melted down for the war effort. There can be no doubt that it was sadly missed by the many children who enjoyed climbing all over it.

THE CITY POLICE COURT, 1904. Known as The Oak Court, this is one of two rooms of justice that were to be found in the Council House at the time. There was also the Council Chamber, the Grand Jury Room, apartments for the Members of the Corporation, a waiting room and a vestibule. The Council room measured 75 feet in length, 24 feet in height, and the same in width.

CELEBRATING THE GOLDEN JUBILEE OF QUEEN VICTORIA, 1897. The sixtieth anniversary of the accession of the Sovereign was a unique event which was celebrated with great enthusiasm by the people of Salisbury. The Council House was generously decorated in red, white and blue. Ribbons were twisted around the portico columns and a large white banner was spread across the roof of the porch, upon which were written, God Save The Queen. Shortly after two o'clock in the afternoon of Wednesday 23 June some 4,500 male persons sat down to dinner in the Market Place, and then at about five o'clock 4,000 women had tea. At dusk the Mayor, Mr Councillor Arthur Whitehead, and Members of the Corporation lead a torchlit procession from Victoria Park, through the city streets, to The Greencroft, where an effective display of fireworks closed the proceedings. This photograph was taken from the roof of the Market House, which is now the Salisbury Divisional Library.

THE COUNCIL CHAMBER AT THE DAWN OF A NEW CENTURY. Taken before 1905, this photograph clearly shows the former position of the Sidney Herbert statue, which was unveiled here in the Market Place on 29 June 1863. On the extreme right of the picture one can see the 50ft wheeled escape ladder that was kept there for many years. It was one of two similar appliances that were too large to fit into the Salisbury Volunteer Fire Brigade station in Salt Lane. The other ladder was parked at the Infirmary.

CELEBRATING THE CORONATION OF KING EDWARD VII, AUGUST 1902. Many of the city's streets were lavishly decorated, but the scene in and around the Market Place was a particularly brilliant one. Being the centre of attention, the Council Chamber was predominantly adorned with scarlet cloth, which contrasted well with the old grey walls. The columns supporting the portico were spirally wound with flowers, and baskets of flowers were hung between the columns. It took on a magical appearance at night, when it was lit up by some ingenious devices that used jets of gas.

CORONATION CARVERS AT THE COUNCIL CHAMBER, AUGUST 1902. Around 4,000 male guests sat down to eat in the Market Place on the occasion of the coronation of King Edward VII. The work of preparing the dinner was divided between three sub-committees, which took charge of the Meat, the Beverage; and the Bread and Pudding. The wants of the

CORONATION
OF
KING EDWARD VII.
CARVERS

diners were attended to by a large staff of stewards. About 150 people helped to keep the beverages flowing, while approximately 250 men carved the meat. Two hundred gallons of bread were consumed, plus 4,250 pounds of assorted meats and 1,600 pounds of plum pudding.

THE SIDNEY HERBERT STATUE ADORNED FOR THE CORONATION, AUGUST 1902. One can see that the pedestal of the statue was completely hidden with a choice collection of colourful flowers and ferns. At night the whole display was set off with an edging of fairy lights. Thirty nine years earlier, on Monday 29 June 1863, the ceremony of inaugurating the memorial was performed by the Earl De Grey and Ripon. Modelled by Baron Marochetti, the 8ft 6in high bronze figure of Lord Herbert of Lea stands on a pedestal of polished Cornish granite. The map that can be seen in his right hand has a plan of the Herbert Memorial Hospital engraved on it. The statue was repositioned in the 1950s, and can now be found looking out over the bowling green at Victoria Park.

THE RECORD SNOW STORM OF 1908. During the early hours of Saturday 25 April a violent storm raged across the south of England. Several Wiltshire villages were completely cut off by deep drifts of snow, and for the first time in thirty years or more a number of country carriers could not get into Salisbury for the Saturday market.

A ROYAL PROCLAMATION, 1910. The accession of King George V to the throne of England was proclaimed in Salisbury on Monday 9 May. Two rows of local territorial soldiers and a military band can be seen here on the gravelled market square. A large crowd of schoolchildren and adults had also assembled to hear the announcement that the Mayor, Mr Councillor Frank Shepherd, was to make from the steps of the Council House.

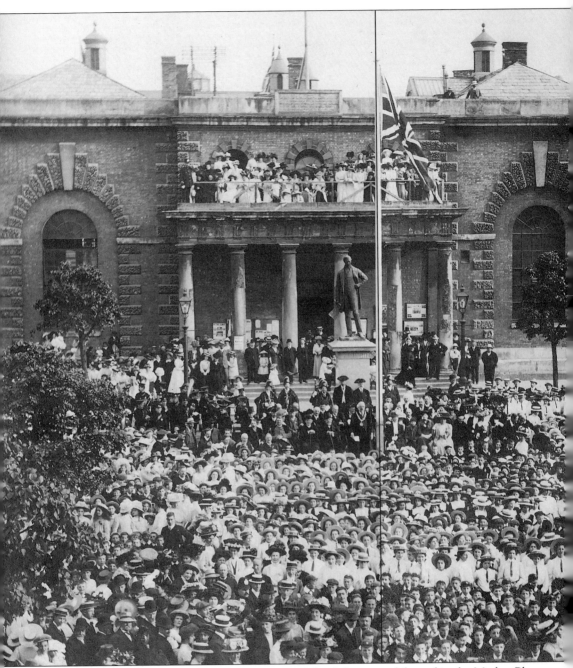

EMPIRE DAY, 1909. The late Queen Victoria's birthday was celebrated in the Market Place on Monday 24 May. It was the first time that the occasion had been observed in Salisbury. Each of the local Council schools was presented with a flag pole and a Union Jack by Lady Hulse, and at 3 o'clock precisely all the flags were unfurled by well-known Ladies and Gentlemen of Salisbury. The children were then entertained to tea at their respective schools, and later they marched to the Market Place for a united demonstration. Approximately 4,000 children attended. The Union Jack that can be seen flying in this photograph was sent to Salisbury in 1907 by the children of Salisbury, New South Wales.

TANK WEEK, 1918. Officially known as War Bond week, the event ran from 4 to 9 March. It was part of a national campaign to raise money for the war effort. The banner that is stretched across the front of the Council House informs the reader that £52,500 was needed for 21 aeroplanes. On the right of the picture one can see the First World War battle tank that toured the city streets on several occasions during the week.

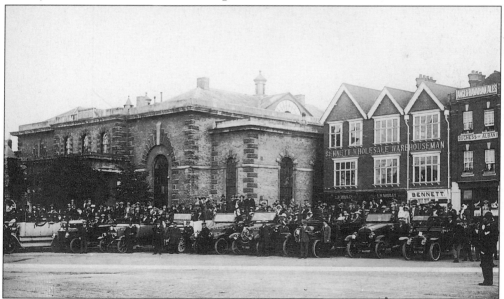

AN OUTING TO SALISBURY IN THE 1920s. A pencilled note on the back of the original photograph suggests that this is a party of Hampshire Hogs. The vehicles are certainly from the Bournemouth area. There are three French-built De Dion Bouton charabancs among them, which are named Lizzie I, Lizzie II and Lizzie III, their registration numbers being FX-2139, FX-1546 and FX-1080 respectively. There are also two Daimlers here from the Royal Blue fleet.

THE INAUGURATION OF SALISBURY WAR MEMORIAL, 1922. The monument was unveiled by Lieut. T.E. Adlam VC on Sunday 12 February. It was dedicated by Revd W.R.F. Addison VC in the presence of the Bishop of Salisbury. Manufactured from Portland stone, and embellished with bronze and marble, the work was carried out by Messrs H.H. Martyn & Company of Cheltenham at a cost of £2,500.

THE COUNCIL HOUSE BECOMES THE TOWN HALL, 1927. At 10 a.m. on 29 June, the Mayor and Mayoress received official guests at the old Council House. A United Service followed at the Cathedral and then there was a civic procession to the new Council House and Grounds (formerly St Edmund's College) at Bourne Hill. The old Council House was known as the Town Hall for just a short time before being officially named The Guildhall. The photograph above shows the floral decorations that embellished the war memorial at that time. The colourful display was created by Hedley Coombs, of 26 & 28 High Street.

COUNTRY BUSES PARKED IN THE MARKET PLACE, MARCH 1923. The Winterslow village carrier's van can be seen on the extreme left. Operated by Edwin Knight, of Shripple Farm, Winterslow, this is a 28hp Dennis, of 1914 (AM-3712). In January 1926 the vehicle was taken over by Reginald Alfred Bell, of Glebe Cottage, Pitton. Next in line is a Thornycroft (AM-9997) which was known as the Victory. This machine covered the Salisbury, Sixpenny Handley and Blandford routes for A. Adams & Son (Cyril) of Sixpenny Handley. The vehicle was sold to a Reading operator in January 1934. The charabanc pictured in the right foreground is the Tidworth bus. It is a 36/40hp Leyland (HR-74) that was purchased by Messrs Bartley and Avery of North Tidworth Garage, Tidworth, in February 1921. It remained in their fleet until April 1929, which is when the firm was taken over by Wilts & Dorset Motor Services Limited. The last road fund licence for this vehicle appears to have been purchased in January 1948. Parked alongside HR-74 is the Royal Red, from Shaftesbury. This is HR-1307, an AEC (type JB4) charabanc that was owned by Frederick M. Rawlings and Reginald Stevens of Victoria Street, Shaftesbury.

THE GUILDHALL DECORATED FOR THE SILVER JUBILEE OF KING GEORGE V,
1935. The colourful display of flags, bunting and crowns that adorned the front of the Guildhall
was undoubtedly a very pleasing sight during daylight hours, but when lit up at night it took on
a truly magical appearance. The building was illuminated by seven lamps of 1,000 candlepower
and four of 2,000 candle power. White and amber beams of light were directed at the porch and
the remainder of the facade was bathed in pink. The floodlighting scheme was devised and
supervised by Cecil Ernest Walters, of 'Wenduyne', Burford Avenue. The installation and
running costs of which were met by his employer, the Salisbury Electric Light Company.

A VIEW OF THE MARKET PLACE FROM THE GUILDHALL PORCH. The photograph shows a Tuesday market taking place in the early 1930s. Numerous livestock pens, poultry coops and produce stalls are set out in the market square. The market traders who occupy the pitches that can be seen here in the Guildhall Square appear to be dealing in linen, clothing and rugs. Motor vehicles and horse-drawn carriages were using the roads at this time.

WHEN THE WORLD WAS AT WAR. The portico, window surrounds, corner stones and columns appear to be painted white at this time. Despite the numerous enquiries that have been made by the author it is still unclear why the building was highlighted in this way. Some individuals will approve of its appearance, but many others would say that it looks hideous.

THE GUILDHALL DANCE TROUPE AT THE TIME OF THE SECOND WORLD WAR.
Pictured from left to right are Monica Bates (later Mrs Goodman), Betty Philips (later Mrs Rigiani), Doreen Simms, Phylis Downs, Josephine Reynolds (later Mrs Mutter), Sheila Hopkins, Heather Simms (later Mrs Pizzey) and Joan Young. Throughout the war years, evening concert parties were staged most Saturday and Sunday evenings from 6.30 to 7.30. The photograph was taken by Reginald Harding, of 38 High Street (formerly Royal Studios).

THE OLYMPIC FLAME ARRIVES IN THE GUILDHALL SQUARE, 1948. Taken during the evening of Sunday 1 August, in the foreground of the picture we can see John Rigiani (left), Derek Babidge and George Chalke, who was Chairman of the Salisbury and District Amateur Athletic Club. He was the County Organiser of this event. Thousands turned out to witness the occasion and the crowd was four deep along Blue Boar Row when the torch arrived. Derek carried the flame from Lopcombe Corner to the Guildhall Square, where it was handed over to John, who then relayed it to Tinkerpit Hill. Torquay was its final destination. John Rigiani was commissioned to an army unit in the Middle East at the time and he was flown home to take part in the run. He was given thirty days leave, which was added on at the end of his service.

CHRISTMAS CAROL SINGING AT THE GUILDHALL, 1951. Large illuminated Christmas trees can be seen on both sides of the porch, and the city's coat of arms is displayed on the wall above the portico. The Mayor of Salisbury, Mr Councillor Sidney Edwin Chalk, and Mrs Chalk were to be seen somewhere among the merry-makers who are pictured here on the Guildhall steps.

RESURFACING THE GUILDHALL SQUARE IN AROUND 1957. An ancient looking excavator can be seen tearing up the tarmacadam surface and dumping it into the back of a Commer tipper truck (GHR 864). The War Memorial appears to be covered with flowers, which does suggest that the above photograph was taken a few days after Remembrance Sunday. The Sidney Herbert Statue can no longer be seen in the square.

Opposite: ONE FINAL LOOK AT THE SIDNEY HERBERT STATUE. This is one of the last pictures that shows the monument standing in its original place in the Market Square. For soon after this photograph was taken the statue was moved to a new spot near the bowling green at Victoria Park. The vehicle parked near the statue on this particular day is an Austin A40 pickup that was owned by Harold James Street, of Ratfyn Farm, Amesbury. Registered on 5 April 1951, the truck was supplied by H. Norman Pitt & Company. HAM 980 is a very suitable number plate for a farmer.

TWELFTH NIGHT DANCE, 13 JANUARY 1961. This annual event usually took place on New Year's Eve. It was organised by the Salisbury branch of NALGO. On this particular occasion around 120 guests were in attendance, with a good turn out of Corporation employees. Among those present was the Branch President, Gilbert Schofield, and Mrs Schofield; the Branch Chairman, Francis Lemon; and the Branch Secretary, John Curtis, and Mrs Curtis. The couple who can be seen dancing in the foreground on the right of the picture are Anne Rhind-Tutt (later Mrs Chalke) and Alan Gordon. There was five hours of dancing to the music of Len Dearlove and his band, from Winchester.

Four

The Photographs of
Austin Underwood

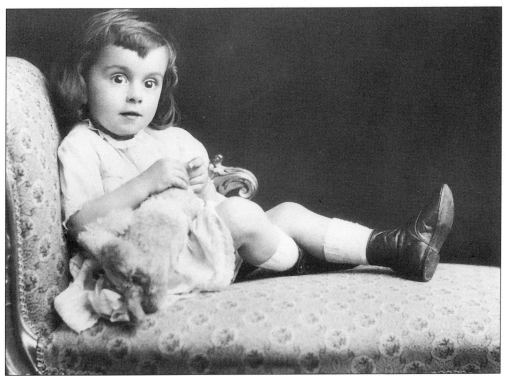

AUSTIN UNDERWOOD, A PHOTOGRAPHIC PORTRAIT BY REGINALD HARDING, 1920. Born at Amesbury on 6 September 1918, he was the son of Frederick William Underwood, a member of the Amesbury Fire Brigade. His mother was Elizabeth Mary, née Laverty, of Winchester. He was educated at Bishop Wordsworth's School, Salisbury; King Alfred's College, Winchester; Lanchester Polytechnic, and Winchester School of Art.

AUSTIN UNDERWOOD, A SELF PORTRAIT. During the early stages of the Second World War, Austin was Section Leader of an A.R.P. rescue unit in London. He then joined the Royal Corps of Signals as a volunteer. He trained as a radio engineer and soon became Foreman of Signals. He was proud to have been one of Field Marshall Montgomery's personal radio officers. The British Empire Medal (Military) was presented to him in 1944. After leaving the army he returned to Bishop Wordsworth's School to run the Department of Design and Technology. He could still be found there thirty years later. A lifetime supporter of the Labour Party, he was elected to the Amesbury Parish and Rural District Councils in 1952. He spent the next thirty-three years of his life working tirelessly for his community. Following local government reorganization in 1974, he served on the Salisbury District Council, and in 1981 he was successfully elected to the Wiltshire County Council. He was an accomplished journalist and photographer, whose work appeared in numerous magazines and newspapers. Having spent the last fifteen years of his life battling against Parkinson's Disease, he passed away on 11 April 1993. He was 74 years of age. He is survived by his second wife, Mary, whom he married in 1953, and their two daughters, Judith and Ruth, who can be seen in the photograph on the opposite page.

JUDITH AND RUTH FEEDING THE·DUCKS AT WEST HARNHAM. Born in August 1955, Judith trained as a teacher. She is now married and lives in South Wales with her husband, Steve Jones, and their three children, Beth, Edwin and William. Ruth, who is a flautist, a music teacher and a painter, was born in December 1957. Her present home is in London. This delightful picture was taken by their father in 1962 or 1963. A medium format Rolliflex camera was used. This is a scene that has been popular since the very dawn of photography almost 160 years ago.

THE MARKET PLACE, OATMEAL ROW AND BEYOND, 1963. A splendid selection of British cars of the 1950s can be seen parked here. The registration numbers on several of them would be very desirable today. Among those to be seen is LAM 789 on a Ford Consul; 5678 MW on a Mk1 Ford Cortina; 6969 MW on a Morris Minor 1000, and 3456 EL on a Wolseley 15-60. A large Jaguar saloon also appears to display the letters PAM. If one car deserves to be singled out, it would be the Humber Super Snipe saloon that is parked in front of the Singer shop, in Oatmeal Row. It carries the registration number SAM 100, which would have a present day value of £5,000 or more. The photograph was taken from a third floor window at Alan R. Snell's shop, at 17 Queen Street.

Opposite: THE SOUTHERN END OF RAMPART ROAD, 1955. This area looks entirely different today. Buildings to the left and right have gone. The houses on the right were demolished in around 1970 to make way for Phase Two of the City Relief Road, which is known as Churchill Way East. The industrial chimney and buildings pictured just left of centre were part of the New Forest Laundry, at 1 Southampton Road. George Diffey & Sons' delivery van can be seen approaching the junction of St Ann Street, Southampton Road and St Martin's Church Street.

A BUSY DAY IN QUEEN STREET, 1938. This photograph is one of several that Austin Underwood produced to illustrate a school project that he was working on. He studied the way in which the City of Salisbury had progressed since the nineteenth century and then went on to create some plans of his own on how it was likely to change in the future. In this photograph we can see the Sebastopol cannon which once stood on a plinth at the east side of the Guildhall.

GIGANT STREET AND THE ANCHOR BREWERY, 1960. The houses shown on the left were demolished some years ago and the Gibbs Mew brewery site was extended to fill the gap. Among the individuals, families and businesses that were to be found on this side of the street in the 1950s are Walter Hinton (number 60), Miss E. Tylee (62A), Mrs Evelyn Anderson (hardware dealer) and C.E. Tylee & Company Ltd (marine store dealers). Also Alex Hounslow (grocer), John Anderson (builder), Ernest Stratford (74) and E.W. Young & Son (timber merchants). The later ceased trading in July 1972, having been situated in Gigant Street for over 100 years.

THE DEVELOPMENT OF QUEEN ELIZABETH GARDENS, 1950s. On the right side of the photograph a sign can be seen which informs the viewer about what is happening here. 'This land is to be developed by Salisbury District Council as Public Walks and Pleasure Grounds. To be known as Elizabeth Gardens to Commemorate the Coronation of Her Majesty Queen Elizabeth II.' The bulldozer pictured in the foreground is filing in the trench that remained after the River Avon was diverted along its present course. Formerly it flowed parallel to, and on the east side of, Mill Road.

ELIZABETH GARDENS, SEPTEMBER 1962. This view clearly shows the new route of the River Avon through the pleasure gardens. In the background, on the left of the photograph, the former greenhouses of Bowling Green Nursery can be seen.

SCOTS LANE, 1957. William Naish's map of Salisbury (1751 edition) shows that this medieval lane was one of the northernmost thoroughfares of the city at that time. It formed the north side of the White Horse Chequer. At the time of this photograph the half-timbered dwelling houses had reached the end of their useful life and they were about to be demolished. The Castle Street Social Club was built to replace them. The last occupiers of the dwellings on this side of Scot's Lane included: Edgar Blake (number 13), William Prangell (17), Archie Cornish (19) and Frederick Whatley (23). Also Mrs L. Hayes (33), Dennis Hayes (35), Stephen Chapman (37), Fred White (39) and Michael McGlinchey (41). The very tall building in the distance is 39 Endless Street, which is where Mrs K.D. Futcher's corner shop could be found.

Opposite: A PANORAMIC VIEW OF THE CITY FROM ODSTOCK ROAD, 1956. The former buildings of the Meyrick Close Welfare Home can be seen on the extreme left of the photograph. These were built in 1878, being part of the Alderbury (later Salisbury) Union Workhouse. Three hundred and forty inmates could be accommodated. In more recent times the establishment was known as Tower House.

FISH ROW IN 1956. The southern facade of the Guildhall can be seen to the right. The buildings to the left were occupied by the following businesses: Ropers (tailor), Wiltons (sports outfitter), Harold Batt (corn merchant), A. Pritchett (butcher), Wheatsheaf Inn (William Rees Jenkins, proprietor) and A. Lewis (tobacconist). Vehicles were permitted here at this time. A British Railway's parcel van can be seen in the distance.

SALISBURY BUSMEN ON STRIKE FOR HIGHER WAGES, 1957. This is one of several photographs that Austin Underwood took on the second day of a week long national bus strike. Among the individuals we believe can be seen standing in this picket line near the Wilts & Dorset Motor Services' garage in Castle Street are Don Bealing, Albert Blackmore, Bill Boniface, Arthur Butt, Maurice Denham, Bill Douthwaite, Alfie Duffin, Jim Foord and Edward 'Knocker' Goddard. Also Ron Morris, George Moxham, Trevor Palmer, Ernest 'Ernie' Parks, Douglas 'Danny' Pearce, Jim Read, Stan Thick, Jim Walsh and Bert 'Woodbine' Williams. Leslie Smith is standing in front of the group, with his hands behind his back. He was a bus driver for thirty-seven years. A wage offer was accepted and the Salisbury busmen returned to work. Twenty-four hours later the Wilts Dorset Motor Services asked the Traffic Commissioner to approve a bus fares rise.

Opposite: THE FAIR CAME TO TOWN, OCTOBER 1957. On the extreme right of this photograph one can see the rear end of a Scammell chain-driven tractor unit that is pulling three trailers. This is Chipperfield's 'Big Wheel' and 'Shooting Gallery' on the move. A small group of spectators had gathered on the corner of High Street and New Street.

AN ALTERNATIVE FORM OF TRANSPORT DURING THE BUSMEN'S STRIKE. Arthur Sainsbury can be seen here near the entrance to the Outpatients' Department at Salisbury General Infirmary. He kindly gave this woman and child a lift in the Ford 5cwt van.

A PAINT JOB ON SALISBURY'S BIG BEN, JUNE 1957. Some splendid roof-top views of the city centre could be seen from the upper floors of Salisbury Infirmary. By studying the left side of this photograph one can clearly see that a number of changes have taken place in this area. The pavement on the north side of the bridge is considerably wider now and some flower gardens and benches have been installed there. An attractive bridge and walkway have been constructed to link Bridge Street, Bishop's Mill (formerly the Town Mill) and The Maltings shopping precinct. The Bristol Lodekka bus (KMW 345) appears to be running on service 64, which covered the route from St Francis Road to the City Centre.

A SNOW CLEARING PARTY AT THE BISHOP'S SCHOOL, JANUARY 1963. A blizzard that swept across the south of England on 29 December 1962 left Salisbury covered in a thick blanket of snow. Several RAF helicopters from the School of Land/Air Warfare at Old Sarum were called out to survey the district. Some villages in Wiltshire were completely cut off and numerous people were left stranded in their cars. The school boys pictured here are clearly enjoying themselves. There were thousands of others around the district who had to stay at home because of their schools being closed.

OFFLOADING SACKS OF BARLEY AT THE MALTINGS IN 1963. The grain had arrived by train from the west of England. The sacks, which bear the name of Bailey & Son Limited of Frome, are being wheeled into a large warehouse. The canopy under which these men walk is seen to the right of the photograph on the opposite page. A large pile of anthracite can be seen in the foreground of this picture. This was used as fuel to fire up the kilns found in all ten of the malthouses. These buildings have now gone and the land is presently occupied by The Maltings shopping precinct and the Central Car Park.

Opposite: THE MALTHOUSES AND THE MARKET HOUSE RAILWAY, 1963. The church of St Thomas of Canterbury and St Thomas' school can be seen in the distance. The full-gauge railway system pictured here was originally constructed for The Salisbury Railway and Market House Company. The tracks were connected to the main line station at Fisherton and The Market House (now Salisbury Divisional Library), which was opened on 24 May 1859. At the time of this photograph the malthouses were owned by H.G. Way and Risdon Beasley Limited, but about a hundred years before that Williams Brothers were the proprietors.

STOKING UP A MALTHOUSE KILN, JANUARY 1963. The photograph to the right shows 66-year-old Bert Phillimore stoking up the furnace with anthracite. Rock sulphur is also thrown onto the flames, from which the heat and fumes rise to sterilize the grain that is scattered on the floors above. Mr Phillimore must have liked his job for he worked at The Maltings for almost twenty years.

AN UNEXPECTED DELIVERY OF COAL IN THE HIGH STREET. The offending lorry is not thought to be the one pictured here. This happens to be a 1943 Austin curtain-sided van that is painted in the once familiar banana yellow colour associated with James Lywood Limited, fruit and vegetable wholesalers of 20a Devizes Road. On this particular occasion they appear to be delivering goods to Hedley Coombs' shop at 40 High Street. Next door is the furniture showrooms of Messrs Shepherd and Hedger (numbers 42 and 44), and nearest to the camera is Mrs M.M. Whitby's establishment, the Crown Hotel. It is not clear what happened to the coal but one can be sure it went up in smoke. The picture was probably taken in around 1959.

Opposite: THE NEW SALISBURY FIRE STATION NEARING COMPLETION, 1964. This complex was built in Ashley Road to replace the original Salisbury Volunteer Fire Brigade station that had been functioning in Salt Lane since 1907. The Cattle Market buildings and Salisbury Cathedral can be seen in the distance.

THE DEMOLITION OF THE SHOULDER OF MUTTON INN, JANUARY 1963. Licensed premises had existed on this site since around 1740. Mr R.N. Dixon was one of the last landlords to serve an alcoholic drink here.

DEMOLITION OF GEORGIAN HOUSES IN BROWN STREET, 17 MARCH 1966. The building on the extreme left of the picture was the home of *The Salisbury Journal* and *Salisbury Times* newspapers. A contemporary Salisbury street directory shows that Alan G. Patients and Edward D. Hopkins were the last occupiers of the two houses shown here (numbers 37 and 39). The Brown Street Baptist Church Institute (built 1908) can be seen to the right of the church. This was demolished in September 1990.

CHILDREN HAVING FUN ON THE GREENCROFT IN THE 1960s. The author spent many a happy hour on these swings in the early 1950s.

A VIEW OVER THE GASWORKS FROM NESTLE'S FACTORY CHIMNEY, 1957. During the closing years of the nineteenth century this area was known as Railway Town because of the large number of railway company employees who lived here. Many of these streets comprise row upon row of Victorian terraced houses.

THE JUNCTION OF ST ANN STREET AND RAMPART ROAD, MAY 1965. The last house on the near side of St Ann Street (number 81) was occupied by Miss Flora Lanning, who was a newsagent. The last house on the opposite side of the road was demolished soon afterwards. This is where the Salisbury Diocesan Association for Moral Welfare was to be found. Miss A. Hatfield was the superintendent.

THE STREET WITH NO NAME, 1961. The thoroughfare from Butcher Row to New Canal has somehow survived for more than 700 years without ever having been given an official name. In Victorian times it was called 'No Name Street' by some, and 'The Pig Market' by others. The latter actually describes the area just out of view to the left of this photograph, which is where Medieval pig markets were held. The space is presently set out as a car park and a village bus park. The Wheatsheaf Inn, which could be found on the corner of the unnamed street and New Canal, has since closed and Sarum Jewellers are there now. The Austin van that can be seen entering No Name Street is finished in the livery of Castle & Company Limited; wine and spirit merchants, formerly of 53 & 55 New Canal.

Opposite: NEW VIEWS AS OLD SALISBURY CRUMBLED DURING THE 1960s. The very heart of the New Street Chequer was removed during the development of the Old George Mall by Hammerson's in 1966/67. A fine, albeit temporary, view of the facades of these early nineteenth-century buildings in New Canal could be seen.

THE GAUMONT CINEMA PROJECTION ROOM, 31 MAY 1967. Ted House, cinema manager, and projectionist Charlie Overton can be seen here. It was not long after their picture was taken that the name of the cinema was changed to The Odeon: At the time of this photograph the Circuits Management Association Limited was the proprietor, and later on, Rank Theatres Limited. There were two cinema entrances in use at this time: New Canal and 28 Catherine Street. The later is no longer used.

Opposite: A SIGN WITH A DOUBLE MEANING. A funeral cortege is pictured here leaving St Osmund's Roman Catholic church in Exeter Street. A Humber hearse is in the forward position, sedately followed by a Daimler limousine and a Humber saloon. The identity of the deceased person is not known to us. The funeral took place on 1 February 1968.

WINCHESTER STREET AFTER THE RAIN, 1967. Shopkeepers fought a battle with flood water on Saturday 24 June, following a thunderstorm of tropical intensity. The torrential downpour caused flooding in a number of city centre streets; 0.61 inches of rain fell during a period of three hours on the Saturday and a further 0.52 inches on the Sunday. Two women are seen here attempting to brush water away from the entrance to Noyce & Sons, newsagents.

MR AND MRS JESSE AT THE DOOR OF THEIR SHOP IN THE FRIARY, 19 FEBRUARY 1969. Mrs Winifred Maud Jesse is pictured here at the age of 79 with her husband William Abel Jesse, aged 80. They had been successfully running this small general store at 73 The Friary since before the Second World War. William's parents, Mr and Mrs John Jesse, were managing it before that. It was originally taken over by the Jesse family in 1889. The shop was open at 7 a.m. every day and it did not close until Mrs Jesse went to bed at around 10 p.m. The couple believed that the customer was king, and whether they were four years of age or 100, they were served tirelessly and courteously, and in a friendly and unassuming manner. The position of the Cathedral spire in this picture should help the reader to understand exactly where the shop was located. This is one of the last photographs of Jesse's shop for soon afterwards it was demolished, along with other neighbouring buildings, in preparation for the council housing development that followed. A different perspective of the shop can be seen in the upper picture on the next page.

Opposite: THE FRIARY AND FRIARY LANE IN THE LATE SIXTIES. The tower of St Osmund's Roman Catholic church can just be seen on the far right of the picture, as well as the back of the Bishop Wordsworth's School that can still be found at 97 Exeter Street. The building in the centre of the photograph is gone and Glastonbury House occupies the site today.

THE JUNCTION OF RAMPART ROAD AND MILFORD STREET, APRIL 1971. The building that can be seen to the right, which was known as St Martin's Hall (the Purvis Memorial), was demolished shortly after this picture was taken. A report in the *Salisbury Times and South Wilts Gazette*, dated 9 December 1966, informed the reader that if the City Relief Road went ahead as planned this listed building would be moved and relocated at the top of St Ann Street, nearer to St Martin's church. The Churchill Way East relief road was built, but the ultimate fate of St Martin's Hall remains a mystery.

THE CONSTRUCTION OF CHURCHILL WAY EAST, 31 MARCH 1972. Phase two of the City Relief Road largely followed the old route of the London Road and Rampart Road, from College Roundabout to Whipping Cross, often mistakenly called Weeping Cross. Known today as St Mark's Roundabout, this was the former location of a whipping post.

Five

Salisbury General Infirmary

THE CLOCK TOWER AND INFIRMARY, 1907. This view was taken from Bridge Street with the County Hotel to the left and Town Mill out of view to the right. A bridge widening scheme in the 1960s necessitated the destruction of the stone wall (right). Attractive flower gardens and benches can be found in this area today. Behind the trees, on the extreme right, one can see the Maundrel Hall, which is now the Salisbury branch of Argos Distributors Limited. The horse-drawn omnibus appears to be one operated by hotel proprietor Edward Wilkes Gawthorne. It was used to carry guests between the railway stations at Fisherton and the Red Lion Hotel in Milford Street.

THE EARLIEST KNOWN PHOTOGRAPH SHOWING THE INFIRMARY, 1874. This remarkable picture was taken soon after the completion of the building shown on the extreme left. Then known as City Chambers, the premises now form part of the County Hotel and Barclays Bank. The construction work got under way in 1872 for Richardson Brothers (wine and sprit importers, shippers and wholesalers), and it continued for two years. Richardson's was the oldest wine and spirit business in the United Kingdom at the time, having been founded in 1625. In the distance one can see the general layout of the original eighteenth-century Infirmary block, and the east and west wings that were added in 1845 and 1869 respectively. The clock tower did not appear until 1893.

Opposite: THE INFIRMARY AT THE DAWN OF A NEW CENTURY. Photographed in 1900, by Horace 'Charlie' Messer, this view shows the main entrance to the hospital. The original building, designed by architect Robert Wood of Bath, was completed in August 1771 at a cost of around £9,000, including furnishings and equipment. Near the top of the front façade one can see the stone frieze on which Mr Macey engraved the following inscription, 'General Infirmary supported by voluntary contribution: 1767'. When an additional floor was added in 1935/36 the frieze was lowered to its present position, which is immediately above the third floor windows.

WILLIAM PINCKNEY, 1905, treasurer of
Salisbury Infirmary and its associated
institution, the Herbert Convalescent
Home, Bournemouth (see illustration on
page 76). The son of Robert Pinckney, he
was born at Amesbury in 1834. Educated at
Eton and Oxford, he later served as a Justice
of the Peace for Wiltshire. Formerly a
partner with Pinckney Brothers ('Salisbury
Old Bank'), at the time of this photograph
he was a director of the Wilts and Dorset
Bank, the two concerns having
amalgamated sometime earlier. He lived at
Milford Hill House with his wife, Frances
Charlotte, the daughter of Reverend G.F.
Everett, of Shaw Rectory, Newbury.

JOHN ROBERTS MD, of the Close Gate, High Street, 1906. The son of Cornelius Roberts, of Dolauen, North Wales, he was born in 1821. Although retired at the time of this photograph, Dr Roberts was a Consulting Physician to the Salisbury Infirmary from 1854 to 1874. He was also founder of the Salisbury and South Wilts Provident Dispensary. He was donor of the Roberts' Hall in the Salisbury School of Art, New Street, and of the illuminated Clock Tower in Fisherton Street, that was built in memory of his first wife Arabella.

THE HERBERT CONVALESCENT HOME, BOURNEMOUTH. Taken on 28 May 1889, this photograph features patients and nursing staff of the establishment in Alumhurst Road, Westbourne that was founded in 1867. The Committee of the Salisbury Infirmary had a claim to fifteen beds for convalescents from that Institution. At the time of the picture the Hon. Medical Attendant was Augustus Edgar Burch Love of 13 Richmond Road, Bournemouth. Miss Lucy Barton was the Matron.

FISHERTON CLOCK TOWER AT THE TIME OF THE FIRST WORLD WAR. In 1892 the Hospital Governors agreed to part with a small plot of land in the north east corner of the Infirmary site, upon which a clock tower was to be built. An area of approximately 800 square feet was sold to Dr John Roberts for the nominal sum of £5. A tablet near the base of the tower bears the following inscription, 'This Clock Tower, commenced in the year 1892 and completed in the year 1893, was presented to the City by Dr Roberts, who erected the same in memory of Arabella, his beloved wife, daughter of Robert Kelham, Esq., of Bleasby Hall, Notts.

MONTAGE OF PHOTOGRAPHS BY MR WITCOMB, 1904. During the early years of the twentieth century, postcards and photographs were very much in vogue, and dozens of local photographers, newsagents and stationers published views to interest patients, staff and visitors of the Infirmary. This selection was displayed in the window of Witcomb & Son, photographers, of 8/10 Catherine Street. The two uppermost images, and the one in the lower right hand corner, depict the Nurses Home that was situated on the corner of Harcourt Terrace and Harcourt Bridge Road (see also page 80). A photograph of the Infirmary chapel occupies the centre position, with Lovers Walk (in Cathedral Close) to the left, and a north west view of the Cathedral to the right. The Clock Tower can be seen in the lower left hand corner.

Opposite: THE INFIRMARY CAB RANK, 1906. The stone-set area in front of the hospital was maintained for the sole use of the horse-drawn cabs that parked there while waiting for fares. During the winter months the cab drivers could warm themselves up in the cabmen's bothy, which could be found next to the public conveniences near the Clock Tower. These facilities can be clearly seen in the photograph reproduced on page 77.

DOCTOR FISON, 1904. Born Edmund Towers Fison on 13 November 1869, he was the son of Cornell Henry Fison JP, CC, of Thetford, Norfolk. Educated at Repton School, Cambridge University, St George's Hospital, London, and the Rotunda Hospital, Dublin, he was later a physician to Salisbury Infirmary. He was also Medical Officer of Health for Salisbury, Medical Officer to the Post Office, and Medical Officer Headquarters Staff Administration Branch, Southern Command. He rowed for Cambridge against Oxford in the years 1890 through 1892. He married Gertrude Mary King, of St Mary's Square, Bury St Edmunds, Suffolk. His house on the corner of St John Street and New Street was demolished and the site was cleared to make way for the new NAAFI Club that opened for business there in November 1955.

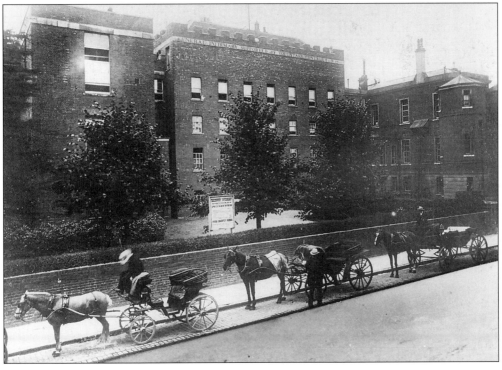

HUMPHREY PURNELL BLACKMORE MD, 1906. A physician to Salisbury General Infirmary, he was also President of the Southern Branch of the British Medical Association. Born in Salisbury on 13 May 1835, he was the third son of William Blackmore, who was Mayor of Salisbury in 1841. He was Hon. Director of Salisbury and South Wilts and Blackmore Museums, President of Salisbury Microscopical Society (founded 1895), and author of the Descriptive Catalogue of Mammalian Remains in Salisbury and South Wilts Museum. For many years he lived at Vale House, 44 St Ann Street, with his wife, Augusta Sophia (second daughter of Colonel Henry Ross Gore CB), whom he married in 1877.

THE FIRST SALISBURY HOSPITAL CARNIVAL PROCESSION, 20 JUNE 1906. Pictured here in Blue Boar Row, on route to a fête at Victoria Park, is the tail end of a procession that was led by the Chief Constable, Frank Richardson, who rode on horse back. He was followed by the event organiser, Frank Baker, who was then Mayor of Salisbury. There were also numerous bands, friendly society banners and decorated carriages. The first prize for a 'Decorated Car' (actually a horse-drawn wagon) was awarded to members of the Harriett Bartlett Female Lodge of Oddfellows. Their entry was entitled 'The Good Samaritans'. A further prize was presented to Messrs Hardy & Son, whose staff had dressed up the firm's Straker steam lorry (AM 426). The exercise was not repeated again until the year 1930.

Opposite: THE SALISBURY INSTITUTE FOR TRAINED NURSES, 1908. Known as the 'Nurses Home', this establishment was situated on the corner of Harcourt Terrace and Harcourt Bridge Road, which is today called Mill Road. Miss Laurence was the Lady Superintendent at the time of the photograph. It was a private institution up until the time of its acquisition by the Salisbury Hospitals authority in the 1940s, when it was renamed the Nurses Preliminary Training School. At the time of writing the building is boarded up and not in use.

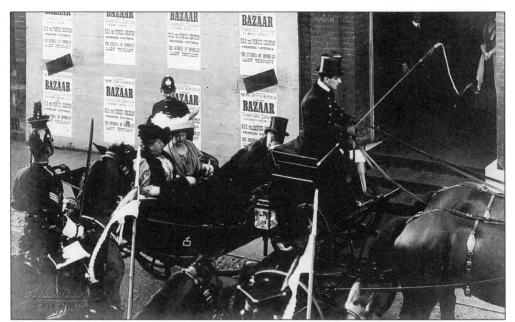

A ROYAL VISIT TO THE INFIRMARY, NOVEMBER 1906. This two-horse landau is parked at the entrance to County Hall, in Endless Street. Princess Christian and her companion, Lady Tennant, can be seen in the carriage. Following their appearance at the official opening of a YMCA bazaar they were driven to the Infirmary. The Princess then walked around the wards to meet members of staff and a number of patients. The picture was taken by professional photographer Horace 'Charlie' Messer of Castle Street, who was also Secretary of Salisbury YMCA.

COLD AND WINTRY VIEW OF THE INFIRMARY, 1908. On 25 April a violent storm swept across the south of England. For almost thirteen hours extremely large snowflakes cascaded earthward and the wind blew fiercely. Deep drifts built up and all the roads and railway lines in and out of the city became impassable. For several hours Salisbury was completely cut off from the rest of the county.

THE VICTORIA HOME FOR NURSES AT THE TIME OF THE FIRST WORLD WAR.
This view across the river Avon, from the grounds of the County Hotel, shows the northern
aspect of the building that was completed in 1901. The construction costs were met by a public
appeal fund that was set up by the Earl of Radnor in 1897, to commemorate Queen Victoria's
Diamond Jubilee. The facility included bedrooms, sitting rooms and several classrooms.

THE INFIRMARY AND VICTORIA NURSES HOME UNDER WATER, 1915. On 15
January millions of gallons of water cascaded into the hospital grounds following a prolonged
period of heavy rain which had caused the Rivers Avon and Nadder to overflow. Parts of
Fisherton Street, the Cathedral, the Close, and West Harnham were submerged to a depth of
fourteen inches. Pleasure boats were taken out of winter storage and put to work ferrying people
up and down Fisherton Street.

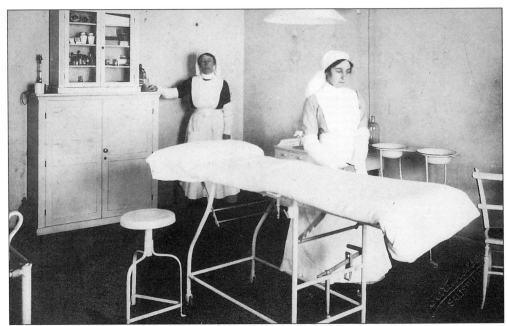

AN EARLY TWENTIETH CENTURY EXAMINATION ROOM. Displayed in the glass fronted cupboard is a selection of bottles and jars containing various medicines and ointments. There also appear to be a few small boxes of medical dressings. On the right, partly obscured by the nurse, one can see a white-painted Victorian wash stand and a free standing unit which holds two enamel bowls. The examination table is fitted with levers and ratchets for adjusting the position of the patient's head and feet.

ON THEATRE DUTY IN THE NINETEEN TWENTIES. The photograph features Nurse Walker and Doctor Alexander. It was produced by Stanley Sutton of 45 Canal.

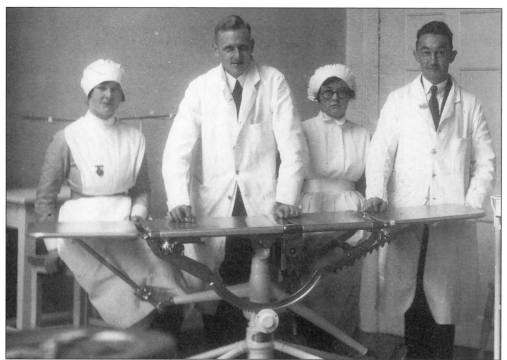

OPERATING THEATRE STAFF AT CHRISTMAS, 1928. Pictured left to right: Nurse Snook, Doctor Gillespy, Sister Whitehead and Doctor Edginton. The surroundings appear to be Spartan compared to the high-tech operating theatres of today.

THE STAFF AND STUDENT NURSES OF BEATRICE WARD, 1930. Pictured in the back row, from left to right, are Nurses Lever, Read, Stocker, Snook and Walker. The Ward Sister can be seen in the middle of the group. Nurses Chant (left) and Hedderman are in the foreground.

SALISBURY HOSPITAL CARNIVAL WEEK, 1930. The Queen of the Carnival, Miss Guendolen Wilkinson, is pictured here in the Market Place with her entourage. She was attended by eight maids of honour – Misses Joan Edwards, Doreen Hopkins, Edith Major, Barbara Sant, Kathleen Sargent, Ruth Sims, Estmin Smith and Barbara Snelgar. Hedley G. Coombs was the herald, Francis U. Pullen, the jester, and Miss Patricia Sant the page.

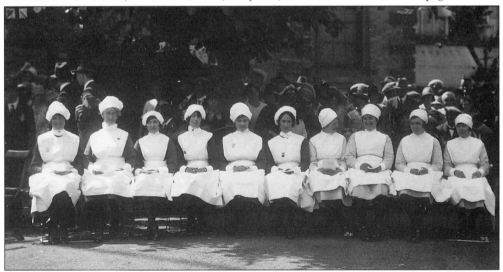

AN AUDIENCE IN THE MARKET PLACE, Monday 30 June 1930. Among those who witnessed the official opening of the Carnival by the Lord-Lieutenant of Wiltshire (the Right Hon. the Earl of Radnor) were ten representatives of the Infirmary. Seated in front of the Guildhall, from left to right, are the sisters of the following wards: Queensberry, Radnor, Feversham, Chafyn Grove, Theatre and Accident. The remaining seats are occupied by Nurses Davy, Mullins, Bath and Stude.

WALTER BATH AND HIS FLYING BEDSTEAD, 1930. This was only the second event of its kind to be held since the Infirmary opened in 1767. The first Hospital Carnival took place in 1906. Salisbury was *en fête* from Saturday 28 June to Saturday 5 July. It was an eventful few days with many attractions, which included Emblem Day (28 June), United Service in the Cathedral (29 June), Carnival Luncheon (30 June), Children's Procession (30 June), Comic Football Match (1 July), Huge Carnival Procession (2 July), Fun Fair at Victoria Park (3 July), Victoria Park illuminated by light, 'Battle of Confetti' (4 July), Torchlight Procession and Community Singing in the Market Place (5 July). Walter Bath, of 36 Sidney Street, is pictured here in the Market Place with his 1927 Austin 7hp tourer (MR 8987), which was decorated with balloons, ribbons and bunting for its participation in the huge procession that was held on Wednesday 2 July. The proceeds from Carnival Week were donated to the new Ear, Nose and Throat Ward which opened on 30 June. A plaque above the door read 'The Carnival 1930 Ward'.

CHRISTMAS CONCERT PERFORMERS, 1930. Pictured from left to right, in the front row, are Nurses Wayling, Harding, Stude, Adcock and Lewis. Nurses Ranger and Rees are in the second row. Nurse Harding can be seen at the back.

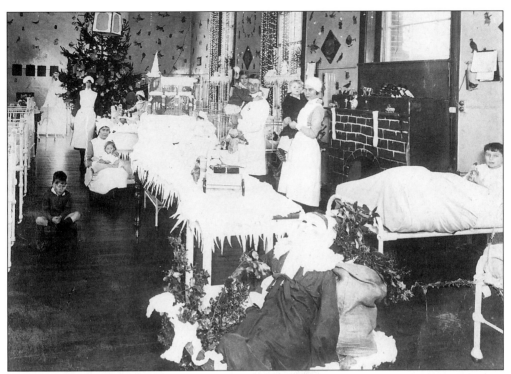

CHAFYN GROVE WARD AT CHRISTMAS, 1931. Geoffrey James Hurford is the 10-year-old boy in the bed on the extreme right of the picture. Nurse Manfield and Doctor Price are standing close by, with two younger patients in their arms. Geoffrey remembers quite clearly the day he needed a transfusion and Doctor Price generously donated a pint of his own blood. He spent fifteen months in the children's ward on this particular occasion, undergoing treatment for osteomyelitis. Geoffrey also recalls how much he enjoyed making the pretty Christmas decorations with cotton wool. This was perhaps one of the experiences of his boyhood that lead him to become a tailor. Following a period of employment with Percy 'Pearly' Adlam (Mayor of Salisbury 1956), Geoffrey set up his own small business in the front room of a house at 40 Rollestone Street. Around forty-four years have passed since then and he can still be seen working away at his sewing machine.

Opposite: THE OUTPATIENTS DEPARTMENT AT CHRISTMAS, 1930. Standing at the back of the group are, from left to right, Nurses Charlesworth and White, the Ward Sister (name unknown) and Nurse Robson (later Mrs Hammett). Nurses Gibbons, Sanger and Hedderman (later Sister Brown) are seated.

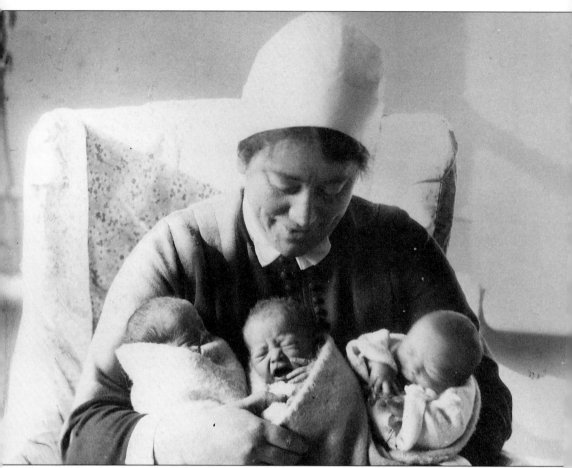

MATRON AND THE TRIPLETS. Pamela, Patricia and Peggy Gates were born in Beatrice Ward on the morning of Wednesday 11 February 1931. They weighed in at 3lb 5oz, 4lb 9oz and 4lb 13oz, respectively. They were the first triplets to be born at the Infirmary during its 165 year history. Nurse Wainwright was the Ward Sister at the time and Miss A.M. Bishop was Matron. There were already six girls in the Gates family before the arrival of the triplets, making Mr and Mrs Walter Gates, of 6 Rampart Road, the proud parents of nine lovely daughters. There were no boys in the family at that time. A few days after the birth of the triplets, Mrs Gates received congratulations from the King, in the form of a King's Bounty. It read 'The Keeper of the Privy Purse is commanded to acknowledge the receipt of Commander J.G. Elgar's letter and to send you a cheque for £3.00 as a donation from His Majesty to Mrs Gates.' Paymaster Commander John G. Elgar DSC, RN (Retired), incidentally, was House Governor and Secretary of the Infirmary from 1928 to 1938. It appears that even during their early adulthood the triplets enjoyed being together, for during the early 1950s they all worked at the Canal and 3 High Street branch of Boots the Chemists.

Opposite: CHURCH PARADE, 1935. Miss Bishop is at the back of the group seen here marching past Herberts ladies' hairdressing salon, which could be found at Mitre House, on the Corner of High Street and New Street (Herberts moved to its present position in Winchester Street in 1950/51). The nurses were on their way to the Cathedral to take part in a thanksgiving service.

PUBLIC APPEAL LAUNCHED TO RAISE FUNDS FOR REBUILDING THE INFIRMARY, 1934. The appeal for £85,000 generated great enthusiasm locally and in the first few months over £1,000 was raised by nursing and domestic staff. This presented an excellent photo opportunity for the Matron (Miss Bishop) and her Staff. Miss Bishop can be seen on the left of the group. She was a strict disciplinarian, whom the nurses rather cruelly named the Green Dragon. Nurse Hedderman stood next to her on this particular occasion.

A CHRISTMAS DISPLAY IN THE ACCIDENT WARD DURING THE EARLY THIRTIES. Sister Judd and Doctor Price stand behind the table, with Nurses Jolly and Robson to the right. The table-top display in front of them represents a hunting scene, with fourteen beautifully made models of riders on horseback (eight adults and six children). There are also twelve hounds to be seen. The hunting theme was not restricted to this corner of the room alone, for the entire ward was decorated with a colourful mural that extended around all four walls. A section of it can be seen in the background. Even the doctors and nurses played their parts; each one had a badge of a rider on horseback pinned to his or her uniform. On several occasions over the Christmas period the male patients in the ward played horse racing games.

Opposite: AUNTIE SMILER WAS AVAILABLE TO ANYONE WHO WANTED HER IN 1935. Assembled by the staff of Salisbury Steam Laundry, as an attraction for Hospital Carnival Week, the mechanical giantess is pictured here in front of the Infirmary. On her first outing, in June 1930, she was attached to the back of a little Austin supplied by W. Goddard & Company of Winchester Street. This gave the impression that Auntie was pushing a pram. Her second major appearance was during King George V's Silver Jubilee celebrations in 1935. Despite a publicity campaign at the time of this photograph, she appears never to have been seen again in public. Her fate is not known.

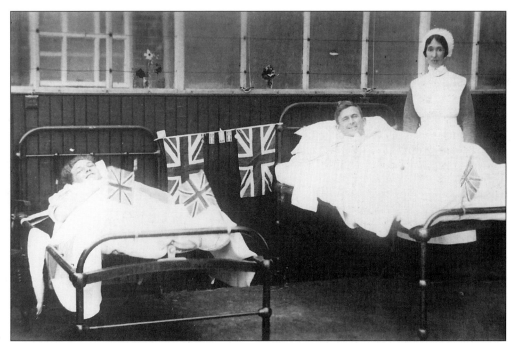

PATRIOTIC PATIENTS, 1935. Depicted here with Sister Judd on the balcony of the accident ward are invalids Harold 'Nobby' Whitworth (left) and Fred Lewis. The photograph records King George V's Silver Jubilee celebrations of May 1935. The picture was probably taken by Nobby's father, Harold Whitworth senior, who was a professional photographer in Salisbury from the end of the First World War until around 1950.

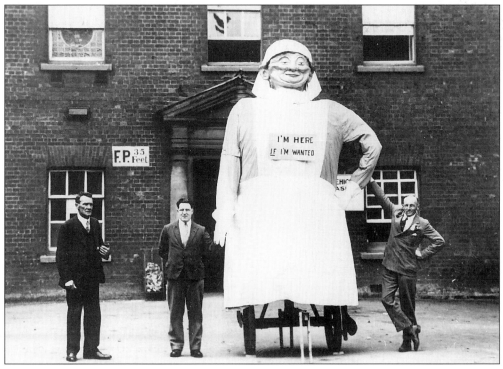

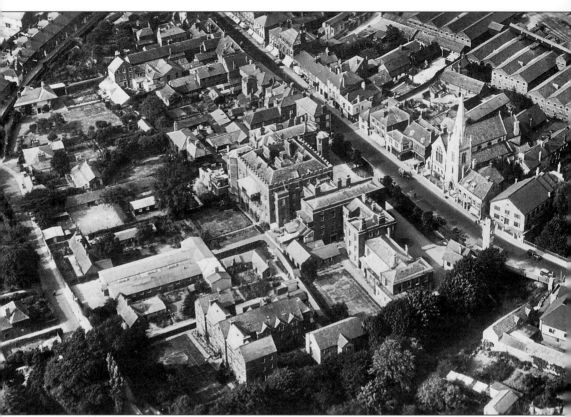

A BIRD'S EYE VIEW OF THE INFIRMARY AND FISHERTON STREET, 1940s. Clearly visible in the centre of the photograph is the original Infirmary block and the numerous extensions that have been built around it over a period of some 180 years. The Victoria Nurse's Home can be seen in the foreground, and, just left of centre, a group of ex-army huts that accommodated the Outpatient's Department. Originally situated in the east wing, the unit was replaced by a new Maternity Department. Motor cars and horse-drawn vehicles could be seen in Fisherton Street at that time. On the right of the picture the Maundrel Hall, Princess Christian Hostel, Congregational Church and Malt House Lane are in view. A close-up photograph of the malt houses is reproduced on page 61.

Opposite: PRIZE GIVING AT THE OUTPATIENTS' HALL, 1950. On 16 December, having completed either one, two or three years of their training courses, the nurses were presented with certificates, badges and prizes. Student nurse Miss Molly Bray is sitting on the floor in front of the group (second from the left). She received a prize for junior nursing, which was a book titled *Wild Flowers of Chalk and Limestone*. This can be seen on her lap. The presentations were made by Lady Radnor, who sits between Miss May Hall, the Matron, and Miss Bulbick, the Senior Tutor.

A POST WAR VIEW OF THE CLOCK TOWER AND INFIRMARY. The photograph was taken from a first floor window at Crown Chambers (14 Bridge Street), which then accommodated the offices of Trethowan, Vincent and Fultons (solicitors), Fletcher, Fletcher and Layton (chartered accountants) and H.T. Jones (solicitor). Compare this illustration with the one on page 73 to see what changes have taken place during the forty years that separate them. The most noticeable differences concern the height of the Infirmary, following its redevelopment in 1935/36, and the cabdrivers' bothy and public conveniences that were situated near the Clock Tower.

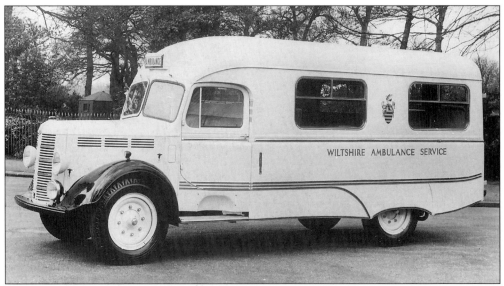

A CITY AMBULANCE OF THE 1950s. Bedford ambulances were very common in Britain during the early post-war years. The example pictured above was equipped with an illuminated 'Ambulance' sign, which was mounted on the roof. It also had an electric bell, a powerful spotlight, a radio telephone and central heating. The appliance shown below was designed to carry five casualties (four seated and one on a stretcher). There was also a seat for a nurse or an attendant. Herbert Lomas, of Wilmslow, and Spurling Motor Bodies, of London, were among the leading ambulance manufacturers at the time.

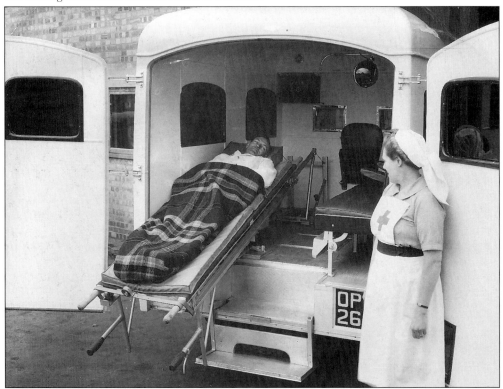

Six

The Second World War

PREPARING FOR WAR, 1939. Police Sergeants Cobden and Stout can be seen supervising the assembly of gas masks in Victoria Hall (12a Rollestone Street). The manager of the Salisbury Steam Laundry stands on the right, at the back of the group. Around 15 April each year the dance floor in this hall was carefully removed to reveal an 80ft by 40ft swimming pool beneath it. Six months later, around 15 October, the floor boards were replaced and the room once again functioned as a concert hall.

A MOUNTAIN OF SAND BAGS AT HIGHBURY AVENUE SCHOOL, 1939. Edward Linzey & Son (builders), of Rollestone Street, was awarded a contract to erect sand bag barriers around a number of local school buildings. This picture shows the work being carried out at the Council School in Highbury Avenue. Fred Allen, Tommy Burton, Frederick Davis, Jim Hunt and Ernie Moody can be seen among the group of labourers sitting above the sign which reads 'Hard up Defence'. A large barrage balloon was tethered in the playground on the far side of the building.

Opposite: NATIONAL SERVICE PARADE IN BLUE BOAR ROW, 24 MAY 1939. The Mayor of Salisbury, Councillor Mr William C. Bridge, can be seen on the right of the picture. Marching past at this point in time is the St John Ambulance Women's Brigade. The officer leading the unit is Mrs E.L. Battye, who appears to be the only individual marching out of step. Marie Maton (later Mrs Knotts) and Rosa Sainsbury are in the foremost ranks.

GAS MASK DRILL AT THE POST OFFICE TELEPHONE EXCHANGE, 1940. The following individuals can be seen among this group of telephonists and telegraphists: J. Bennett, J. Pyle, B. Beckley, Winifred Vickery (later Mrs Stacey), Nora Sherwood (later Mrs White), B. Brewer, J. Eyles, M. Moody and Edna Carnell (later Mrs Pittman).

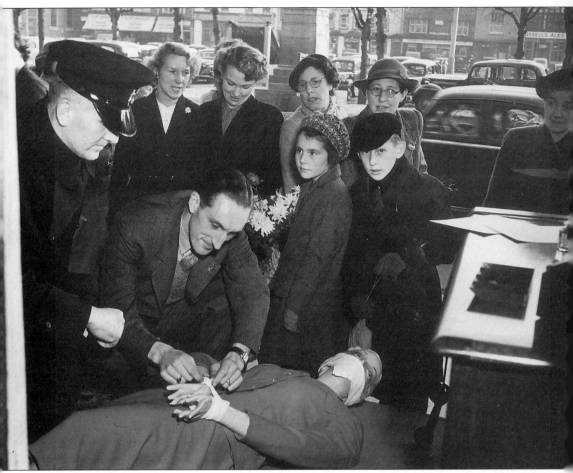

A FIRST AID DEMONSTRATION, 1939. The women and children peering through the display window at Style and Gerrish's emporium (now Debenhams) in Blue Boar Row seem to be quite interested in the first aid demonstration taking place there. Sergeant Cobden, of the Salisbury City Police, stands on the left. The gentleman making the presentation appears to have bound and gagged the mannequin. A glimpse into the background of the picture shows that mostly Austin, Ford, Hillman and Vauxhall cars are parked in the Market Place. Canvas canopies are draped over the entrances to the ladies and the gentleman's conveniences.

THE FILLING OF SANDBAGS IN ENDLESS STREET, 1939. The building that is being protected against an attack from the enemy is the Salisbury City Police Station in Endless Street, which is now Castle Cameras (opened here in 1985). The station also functioned as the Air Raid Precautions Office. Police Constables Hutchings and Wilding were on spade duty this particular day.

QUEEN MARY'S VISIT TO SALISBURY, 23 APRIL 1940. Her Royal Highness can be seen on the extreme right of the picture, which was taken on St George's Day. The passing ranks are those of an Auxiliary Territorial Service unit that was based in the Close. More than 200 individuals marched along North Walk to salute the Queen. Her Majesty then dined at the Theological College (pictured left) with her host, Major J. Despencer-Robinson MP.

A LOCAL DEFENCE VOLUNTEER, 1940. The photograph depicts Geoffrey Gilbert, who lived formerly in Shirley, Croydon. He moved to Salisbury and became manager of T.T. Johnson Opticians, at 17/19 Catherine Street (originally at 59 Catherine Street). He remained with the firm until the time of his retirement in 1977. At the beginning of the war Mr Gilbert signed up as a private in a Mobile Column of the 7th Wilts Battalion Home Guard. After five years he came out as a Lieutenant. This photograph was taken at the front door of his house at 4 Kent Road, which was built in 1939 (No.4 is now No.11). Mr Gilbert is married to Ethel (née Murkett). They have two sons, Peter Jeremy and Geoffrey John.

AN AUXILIARY FIRE SERVICE RECRUITMENT DRIVE, 1941. Pictured here heading in an easterly direction along Winchester Street are two Auxiliary Fire Service dispatch riders. The motorcycle on the right is a Royal Enfield 250, which is ridden on this occasion by Henry Percy Topham, who then lived at 434 Devizes Road. F.G. Usher's shop (No. 14) is now the office of Bennetts Motor Insurance. Hills and Rowney (picture frame makers) were at number 12, which is now M.F. King's, the dispensing chemist. The YMCA building, which can just be seen in the background, has gone. It is now the entrance to the Cross Keys Chequer shopping mall.

Opposite: A 7TH WILTS BATTALION HOME GUARD RECONNAISSANCE UNIT, 1941. From a basement office in Culver Street this Mobile Column covered the outlying areas of Salisbury. Their vehicles were kept at Wessex Motors Garage in New Street. General Sir Geoffrey Brooks was their Commanding Officer. Pictured here with an Ariel motorcycle and an armoured Hillman car is dispatch rider, Harold Keith Trevallion, of West Harnham. Private Nicholas and Private Pole are also depicted. Geoffrey Gilbert is at the back of the group.

AUXILIARY FIRE SERVICE PERSONNEL IN THE GROUNDS OF THE WHITE HART HOTEL, SEPTEMBER 1941. Pictured, left to right, in the back row: S.R. Denham, W.E. Chalk, F.J. Long, G.R. Siggery, D.E. Neale, G.R. Lansdale, O.F. Noyes, G.J. Chamberlain, C.B. Ralph. In the middle row: P.R. Heelas, J.W. Cooke, D.C. Poulton, G.G. Hayward, S. Hedden, H.T. Evans, W. Earney, J.F. Bennett. In the front row: R. Young, R.T.S. Taylor, A.T. Grammer, C.W.H. Roles (4th Officer), A.A. Maidment (Sub-Officer), C.N.E. Hunt, S.W. Edwards. This is one of two photographs taken by Mr Futcher on 23 September. The second view shows the firemen wearing tin hats.

Opposite: A SELF-PROPELLED HEAVY FIRE PUMP UNIT. Based on the Fordson 7V chassis (V8 Engine), this is a typical Second World War fire appliance. Manufactured to government specifications this one was put to work in June 1941. It is painted grey with National Fire Service (NFS) markings. At least four of these fire engines were based in Salisbury, two of which were garaged at Quidhampton. This is now a preserved appliance.

AUXILIARY FIRE SERVICE PUMP DRILL, 1941. The firefighters pictured here were based at No.1 Auxiliary Fire Station, which could be found on the former Walls ice cream depot near the junction of Devizes Road and Gas Lane. C.N. Higgins was the Section Officer. During this particular exercise the men were to draw water from the River Avon. A length of suction hose is being dropped into position. The trailer pump was transported here by an Austin Auxiliary Towing Vehicle (ATV). The Castle Street boathouse can be seen in the background.

AIR RAID PRECAUTION WARDENS. The picture was taken in front of number 14 Wilton Road, which was the residence of Frederick Cutmore, a dentist. A note on the reverse side of the original photograph reads, 'To Senior Warden Harding, with Compliments from No.1 District Warden.' Among those depicted are Messrs Cope, Courtney (Mayor of Salisbury, 1945), Henbest, Marsden (shop proprietor, of 12 Devizes Road), Rogers, Scadden, Voce and Wise.

A DELIGHTFUL VIEW OF SALISBURY CATHEDRAL FROM WEST HARNHAM, 1943.

Opposite: VERY LITTLE TO LOOK AT IN THE CATHERINE STREET SHOP WINDOWS. Permanent Waving and Violet Ray Treatment are highlighted in the Maison Trump shop window. Salisbury Hi-fi is there now (opened in 1986). T.T. Johnson (Opticians) Limited are at numbers 17 and 19. Their original Salisbury outlet was at 59 Catherine Street, which opened in 1911. The Café Rendezvous (F. Beasley, proprietor) was at number 21. Harris & Sons (ironmongers) were to be found in the mediaeval timber-framed building, which sadly no longer exists. The Liberty shop occupies its modern replacement.

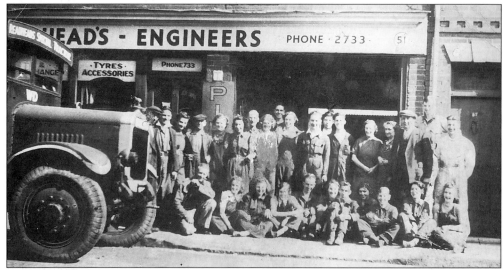

READHEAD'S ENGINEERS, BROWN STREET, 1942. F.R. Readhead's motor engineering works was situated at numbers 51, 53 and 55 Brown Street. The building was demolished after the war and the Brown Street coach park can now be found on the site. The following individuals worked here at the time of the Second World War: Kathleen and Lydia Eggleton, Gladys Webb, Doris Whapshare (later Mrs Ruffell), Bill Chick, Freddie Dear, Fred Fulford, Sydney Hart, Ken Read and Mr R. Lane. Mr and Mrs Frank Readhead can be seen standing near Mrs Norris (forewoman) on the right of the group. Readhead's Special Tractor (a Thornycroft) is depicted left.

EMERGENCY MEDICAL SERVICE STAFF AT TOWER HOUSE. Nurse Phyllis Maud Coggan (née Osmond), of Stratford-sub-Castle, stands in the back row, sixth from the right. She was one of several doctors and nurses who were sent to the Southern Railway Station, at Fisherton, to meet the trains that brought back sick and injured soldiers from Dunkirk. At the time of this photograph Tower House was officially known as the Salisbury Institution. It was situated on land now occupied by the Ridings Mead housing estate.

A FEW MOMENTS OF PLEASURE IN A CRAZY WORLD. Around thirty adults appear to be peering over Fisherton Bridge to catch a glimpse of a pair of swans and nine cygnets swimming in the river below. The Church of England Institute (Maundrel Hall) can be seen in the background. The small building depicted to the left is a public convenience which has not survived. Here, women were accommodated at street level, while the gentlemen had to go underground.

HEATHER LANGFORD AND LEN WATTS TRYING ON THEIR GAS MASKS. Heather's home was at 50 Trinity Street. Her grandfather, Charles Thomas Langford, was proprietor of a cycle shop at 57 Winchester Street. Born on 24 June 1938, Len lived at 102 Love Lane with his mother, Olive Watts (née Lee), and his younger brother, Norman. Their father, Stanley, was killed while on active duty in Italy. Heather is wearing a conventional type of gas mask, which was intended for older children. Len's example was designed for the younger ones. It is known as the Mickey Mouse mask. The picture was taken in the back yard of 102 Love Lane.

A SALISBURY WARTIME NURSERY. In the early days of the war, two prefabricated buildings were erected on the College Street green, which is where the Salisbury Swimming Pool complex can be found today. The unit provided day care for the children whose mothers were out working in the factories. Joan Burton (later Mrs Barnard) was a Care Assistant at the time of this photograph. The following children are thought to have attended the nursery: Tony Brown, Tony Downer, Peter and Geoffrey Gilbert, Barry Cancel, Laurence McGowan and Beverley Hughes.

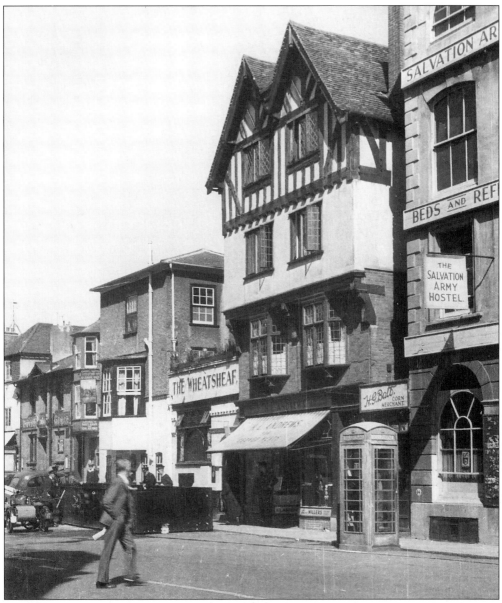

AN EMERGENCY WATER SUPPLY IN THE CANAL. A large metal water tank can be seen on the left of the picture. It appears to be positioned in front of Harry Andrew's grocery store, at 4 Canal. It bears the number 35, which may be an indication of the number of similar containers to be found around the city at the time. In an emergency the tanks ensured that an immediate and easily accessible supply of water was available to firefighting crews. This was essential due to the large number of National Fire Service appliances that did not carry water. During the early post-war years, numerous changes took place in this part of the street: the name of the thoroughfare was officially changed from Canal to New Canal. Harry Andrews gave up selling groceries and Ye Galleon Snack Bar was opened. The Salvation Army Hostel (Major and Mrs Ernest Ward in charge) is now Supersnaps (opened 1974). Rowland's, of Bath, now trade in the premises of the former Wheatsheaf Inn. The rear entrance of H.T. Batt's corn merchant's shop is now The Tea House, of Covent Garden.

THE MAYOR AND THE PRINCESS, 1943. Pictured here on the steps of the Guildhall during an official visit to the city is the Duchess of Kent, Her Royal Highness Princess Marina. Her escort on this occasion was Councillor Mr Ernest Railton Grant, Mayor of Salisbury, details of whom can be read on the next page. The Princess was widowed a few weeks earlier. Her husband, Prince George, was killed in a flying boat accident in Scotland on 1 August 1942. He was flying in a Sunderland that was en route to Iceland.

THE MAYOR OF SALISBURY, COUNCILLOR MR ERNEST RAILTON GRANT, 1943. The son of Austin Benjamin Grant, he was born in Salisbury on 9 May 1891. Educated at St Thomas's School, he later served as a Justice of the Peace of the city. He first became interested in local politics in the 1930s, when he stood as the candidate for the St Edmund's Ward. Despite being defeated on that occasion he was later elected as the representative of the St Mark's Ward, which is a position he held for many years. He was invested as the 694th Mayor of Salisbury at a Luncheon held at The Guildhall on Tuesday 9 November 1943. He lived at 'Torridge' (5 Albany Road) with his wife Elsie May, the daughter of William Bartlett of 33 Rampart Road, Salisbury. They had two children: Paul John and Claire Jean (later Mrs Burroughs).

ST PAUL'S WARTIME SUNDAY SCHOOL FESTIVAL. Led by the Junior Salvation Army Band, a group of local children can be seen marching along St Paul's Road in the direction of the church. John Pothecary and Kenneth Knee (now deceased) are carrying the banner, which still exists. Among the children walking behind them are David Footman, Gwen Hall and Betty Knee. Also Vera Restall, an evacuee from Portsmouth, who was billeted with the Larcombe family at 3 Kingsland Road. In procession behind the children were the teachers, Misses B. Bevis (Mrs Butler), V. Chandler (Mrs Lakeman), M. Hammond and E. Larcombe (Mrs Sherwood).

BETTY AND URSULA ON MAINTENANCE DUTY, 1942. Seen here while working on the engine of a Vauxhall car are Betty Stud and Ursula Lewis, who were both members of a local unit of the Women's Transport Service. This was a government department that managed the driving and maintenance personnel of light soft-skinned military vehicles, such as ambulances and staff cars. Introduced in 1909 as the First Aid Nursing Yeomanry, the service continued unchanged until the year 1933, when it was renamed the Women's Transport Service. Any individual member of this unit is known as a FANY, which is an abbreviation of First Aid Nursing Yeomanry. Several of those stationed in the Salisbury area were billeted at Milford Hill House. Diana Channer (later Mrs Drummond) was one of them. Were a list to be made of the important people she has driven around in her army staff car, the names of Richard Dimbleby and Henry Lamb (an artist) would be included.

Opposite: THE WORK OF WESSEX MOTORS LIMITED. Messrs Bright and Lawrence were the founders of The Salisbury Garage, which had offices at 60 Catherine Street and a workshop in Friary Lane. Following a takeover at the time of the First World War, the company changed its name to Wessex Motors Limited. In the 1920s and 1930s many types of cars and vans were sold and serviced. During the Second World War the firm maintained thousands of War Office vehicles. This four-wheel-drive Humber ambulance was the 1,000th government vehicle to be repaired at the firm's workshop, which was then to be found in New Street.

THE AUSTIN LIGHT LORRY, A WORKHORSE OF THE BRITISH ARMY. Mr R.J. Hogan (Works Manager) and Len Johnson (Storeman) are among the individuals pictured here with an Austin 40cwt General Service truck. This was one of the most common types of military vehicles to be sent to Wessex Motors during the war, be it for the repair of bodywork or mechanical parts. The photograph was taken by J. Fowler Smith.

SALISBURY WARDENS WHO WERE SENT TO WIMBLEDON IN 1944. Units of the Salisbury Civil Defence were sent to Wimbledon several times during the war to relieve the London Air Raid Wardens. It was a frightening experience for them, being billeted in a large school which had many windows. The following wardens appear in the photograph, in the back row, left to right: F.D. Venn, A.E. Coe, D.W.G. Bennett, D. Farrar, R. Jackson, H.C. Rockett, L. Trimbie, R. Dawkins, J. Tilley. Second row: F. Sharp, S. Sutton, C. Blake, H. Sowden, Major M. Rawlence DSO, JP, W.G. Noakes, E.P. Adlam, D. Targett, J.B. White, W.J. Hartley. Front row: Major E. Wallace, Mrs A. Martin, Mrs D. Bartlett, Mrs G. Harris, Captain G.N. Rawlence MC (Chief Warden), Mrs H. Boyd, Miss K.M. Ellaby, P. Bates, W. Noyce, C. Davis.

Opposite: THE SCENE IN FISHERTON STREET. George Chandler of 5 Sidney Street can be seen on the left, passing Gullick's (florists) shop. He is walking along with Peter and Geoffrey Gilbert of 4 Kent Road, West Harnham. Their father, Geoffrey Gilbert senior, was manager of T.T. Johnson Opticians in Catherine Street. Although photographic film was in very short supply at the time, Geoffrey did manage to find a couple of spare rolls. He then toured the city streets to take photographs of the celebrations with a 35mm Leica camera. Both the pictures on page 117 are his, plus several others that follow.

CELEBRATING VICTORY IN EUROPE, 1945. This was the scene in Catherine Street on V.E. Day, Tuesday 8 May. The people walking in the street have smiles on their faces and Union Jacks adorn many of the buildings. There is, however, just one reminder of the passing era: the Bedford 15 cwt army truck which is parked outside McIlroy Brothers' shop.

A CIVIC AND MILITARY PROCESSION, LED BY THE CITY MACE. A thanksgiving service was held at the Cathedral on Sunday 13 May 1945. It was attended by civil and military officials and members of the public. Jock Kerley can be seen carrying the City Mace as he enters High Street from Silver Street (known as Snook's Corner). He is followed by the Mayor (Councillor Mr Frederick Courtney), the Mayoress (Mrs Courtney), members of the Corporation and representatives of His Majesty's Services. In the afternoon a march-past took place in Blue Boar Row (see below).

FLAGS AND PENNANTS DECORATE THE HIGH STREET. The city was alive and there was a great feeling of well-being. People stood around on street corners chatting to each other. GIs could be seen everywhere. Several American GMC army trucks were decorated and driven round and round the streets. Church bells rang. Railway engine whistles blew and sirens were sounded. The Salvation Army Band played dance music in the Market Place. There were three unofficial bonfires in the Guildhall Square. Many of the city centre streets were gaily decorated in red, white and blue. Numerous Union Jacks and other allied flags could be seen in High Street – at Herbert's (hairdressers), Citizens Advice Bureau, Turner's (grocers), Crown Hotel, Moonraker Restaurant, Beach's (book shop), Harding's (photographers), Sutton's Restaurant, Old George Hotel, Hamblin's (opticians) and others.

Opposite: THE WILTSHIRE REGIMENT BAND ENTERTAINS, SUNDAY 13 MAY 1945. Shortly after this photograph was taken a grand parade proceeded along Blue Boar Row. At 3 p.m. precisely the first units of military and civil service personnel marched past the Mayor, who stood at a saluting base at the foot of the Fawcett statue.

FREE ICE-CREAMS FOR THE CHILDREN IN MEADOW ROAD ON V.E. DAY, 1945.
This was the scene outside E. Rigiani & Son's shop at 50 Meadow Road, during the afternoon
of Tuesday 8 May. Mrs Rigiani can be seen here generously handing out free ice-creams to the
children. Her family held the local franchise for Coca-Cola, which no doubt helped the firm to
succeed during the lean war years. Thousands of bottles of the popular drink were consumed by
the countless American citizens who were to be found around Salisbury and South Wiltshire at
that time.

Opposite: A FEW WORDS FROM THE MAYOR AT THE SIDNEY STREET PARTY.
Councillor Mr Alfred 'Fred' Courtney and his wife, Nora, hoped to visit every street party in the
city. They were accompanied by Councillor Sidney Edwin Chalk and his wife. Mrs Courtney is
the woman pictured just left of centre. She is holding a cup of tea. Mr Chalk is the gentleman
seen standing by the side of the car, which has a union flag draped across its roof. He was Mayor
of Salisbury for the years 1951 and 1952. Mrs Clark can be seen on the right. Her son was later
Mayor of Wilton.

ABSOLUTE VICTORY FOR THE LUCAS FAMILY. The celebrations in the area of Meadow Road, Sidney Street and York Road were perhaps the most lively in the City. Several road races were held in Sidney Street as a part of their street party. Here we can see the mothers' race in progress, which was won by Mrs Lucas. Mr Lucas was victorious in the fathers' heat and Carole Lucas was first across the finishing line in the children's race.

SIDNEY STREET CHILDREN'S TEA PARTY, V.E. DAY. Carole Lucas is the child pictured nearest to the camera. The youngster seated in the highchair is John Kingswell and to his left is a girl named Pat. She was a Portsmouth evacuee. The woman standing on the left of the photograph is Mrs Ivy Card (née Weeks). Tony Wright is seated on the right with his mother standing behind him. She is wearing a light coloured dress and has dark hair.

FANCY DRESS FUN FOR A FEW CHILDREN IN YORK ROAD ON V.E. DAY. Pictured left to right: Lou Johnson, Sheila Bariffi, Enid Shearing, Jean Elliott and Shirley Carey.

THE PARK STREET PARTY ON V.J. DAY, 1945. The residents of this street were joined by revellers from several neighbouring thoroughfares, including College Street, London Road and Queens Road. During the war the following families lived in the houses depicted above: Smith (number 42, far right), Abel (44), Arnold (46), Cane (48), Tutt (50), White (52), Trapp (54), Hayman (56, far left). Another photograph of the Park Street party appears on the next page.

A GATHERING OF THE PARK STREET REVELLERS ON V.J. DAY, 1945. The following list is not a complete record of the individuals pictured above. June Able, Mr Able, Mr Beavans, Betty and David Dibden, Alan Franklin, Rhona Hann, Betty Hardy, Margaret Hardy, Jack Harrison, Jean Hayman, Betty and John Hayward, Molly Hayward, Dora and Bob Kelsey (Portsmouth evacuees), Grace May, Jack and Alan Merriman, Barbara Mott, Beryl and Doreen Newell, Mrs Paxman, Diana Rogers, Barbara Singleton, Mrs Skutt, Mr Stent, Roy Sturgess, Janet, Barbara Tutt, John and Olive Tutt, Kenneth Tutt, Joan Walker, J. Wheble, N.A. Wheeler, Zoe Wheeler (Old Mother Reilly), Vic Wiltshire.

Salisbury Commercial Photographers

John Arney	43 Castle Street	1889-1890
Arney and Son	Victoria Studio, 29 Castle Street	
	(also at North Street, Wilton)	1891-1896
Harry Brooks	45 High Street	1897-1926
Henry Brooks	60 High Street	1858-1917
F. E. Brooks, Mrs	60 High Street	1880-1926
Theodore Brown	Portland House	
	(on junction of Wilton/Devizes Roads)	1898-1903
	34A Castle Street	1903-1906
	Nelson Road	1902-1906
Henry G. Buckle	71 New Street	1910-1912
	3 Dews Road	1912-1921
Camera Corner	16 Winchester Street	1931-1936
(J. Fowler Smith, proprietor)		
Collins (G) and Morgan	42 Rollestone Street	1890s
Conduit Photographers	6 Bridge Street	1949-1953
	31 Devizes Road	1953-1959
Whitfield Cosser & Co.	80 Castle Street	1905-1914
(also at Bath, Colchester, Devizes, King's Lynn, Ipswich, Southampton)		
Alfred Dunmore	Wilton Road	1875-1878
	117 Fisherton Street	1878-1880
	London Road	1880-1881

Eastmans, Castle Studios (Philip S. Eastman, proprietor)	29 Castle Street	1920-1957
Thomas Edwards	30 St Ann Street	1864-1885
W. T. Ellis	1 Dews Road	1920s
	Churchfields	1930s
Q. Erdington & Co.	address unknown	1910s
Falcon Studios	4A Endless Street	1949-1953
H. J. Foley	86 Fisherton Street	pre-1900
F. Futcher & Son	19 Fisherton Street	1905-to date
(Frederick Futcher originally at 36 High Street, Warminster)		
C. P. Gearing	High Street	1867-1868
Hall & Co.	Second Floor, Midland Bank Chambers, Market Place	1925-1926
Reginald W. Harding (formerly Royal Studios)	38 High Street	1939-1945
James W. E. Henderson	79 Queen Alexandra Road	1931-1932
	35 St Andrews Road	1932-1936
Ernest Hopkins	address unknown (later moved to Gillingham)	1890s
E. Leman	Queen Street	1867-1868
	Fisherton Street	date unknown
Herbert Light	79 Winchester Street	1913-1915
M. Macey, Mrs	Second Floor, Midland Bank Chambers, Market Place	1925-1932
E & N Macey	40 Fisherton Street	1930-1938
Edwin Macy	Wiltshire Photographic Rooms, Town Mill House, St Thomas' Churchyard	1865-1880
Horace Charles Messer	29 Castle Street	1896-1920
James Wesley Miell	21 Catherine Street	1859-1867
(Photographers to The Royal Family)		
	45 Catherine Street	1867-1880
	West End Studio, Fisherton	date unknown
Ivy B. M. Mortimer, Miss	Second Floor, Midland Bank Chambers, Market Place	1923-1927
Muir Martin Jnr.	37 Blue Boar Row (Polyphoto)	1944-1959
Bertram S. Mullins	80 Castle Street	1914-1923
Neville	High Street	1865-1866
James Owen	Audley House, Crane Street	date unknown
	29 Catherine Street (also at Union Street, Andover)	1878-1896
F. Owen, Mrs	29 Catherine Street	1896-1903
Photokraft	112 Fisherton Street	1942-1959
William Thomas Pitcher	St Ann Street	1859-1860
Marlo Rewse	133 Exeter Place, Station Road, Fisherton	pre 1889

Harry Marlow Rewse	133 Fisherton Street	1889-1895
	163A Fisherton Street	1895-1900
	131 South Western Road	1900-1906
	25 Water Lane	1906-1930
Ritchie	address unknown	1920s
B. E. W. Roberts	23 High Street	1950-1953
Edmund Rogers	De Vaux Place	1865-1879
Marian Rogers	De Vaux House, The Close	1879-1905
Royal Central Photo. Co.	38 High Street	1892-1919
(James E. Jarvis, proprietor)		
Royal Studios	38 High Street	1919-1939
(Reginald W. Harding, proprietor)		
George F. Sands	45 Canal	1911-1939
Edward Wynne Sanger	Devizes Road	1878-1885
Scotford Limited	6 Queen Street	1920-1923
J. Fowler Smith	4 Blue Boar Row	1936-1940
	47 Catherine Street	1940-1944
	45 Canal	1944-1953
	23 High Street	1953-1959
(J. F. Smith was employed at Eastman's before 1936)		
J. B. Stokes	27 Milford Street	
	(also at 12 New Road, Southampton)	pre 1900
Stanley Sutton	45 Canal	1919-1944
Edward John Target	79 Winchester Street	
	(New School of Photography)	1878-1880
	45 Catherine Street	1880-1886
	79 Winchester Street	1886-1912
Charles Taylor	Wilton Road	1865-1866
Frederick Treble	14 Catherine Street	1861-1867
Charles Turner	83 Castle Street	1903-1904
Harold Whitworth	3A St Ann Street	1919-1920
	49 New Street	1920-1931
	15 Meadow Road	1931-1950
Charles John Witcomb	Milford Street	1862-1867
Witcomb & Son	47 Catherine Street	1867-1872
(son was Sydney George)	10 Catherine Street	
	(also at 9 Triangle Bournemouth	
	and Silver Street Warminster)	1872 1886
	8/10 Catherine Street	1886-1909
Frank Sydney Witcomb	53 Canal (also at Yeovil)	1918-1925
(son of Sydney George)	16A Catherine Street	1926-1942
W. D. Yeates	Ye Old Gate House, 92 Winchester Street	pre 1920

Acknowledgements

It has been a great pleasure and a privilege to have met so many interesting people during the twenty years or so that I have been researching the social history of Salisbury and its environs. It would be quite impossible to name each and every one of you in the limited amount of space that is available here, so I have restricted the list of acknowledgements to those individuals and organisations who have contributed to this particular work. My apologies to those who have supplied material that has not been used this time.

I am especially grateful to Mrs Mary Underwood for allowing me to reproduce a selection of photographs that were taken by her late husband, Austin. The quality and content of his work is clear for all to see.

My thanks also to Judith Giles and Bruce Purvis, of the Salisbury Local Studies Library; to Graham Fry, Anita Goddard and Graham Payton, of The Guildhall, Salisbury; to all the members of staff at the Wiltshire Record Office, Trowbridge; to Angela Turnbull, the Features Editor of the *Salisbury Journal*; to Dave Humphries of the *Western Daily Press*; plus the following individuals: Joan Barnard, Elizabeth Batten, Bill Biss, Jackie Brice, Miss Molly Bray, Janet Brown, Barbara Burton, Anne and Peter Chalke, George Cobden, Patrick Coggan, Jan Collins, Ann Crow, Frederick Davis, Mrs M. Dawkins, Diana Drummond, Mrs V. Easter, Tony Futcher, Geoffrey Gilbert, Vic Gill, Peter Grant, Daphne Greville-Heygate, Mrs A Hammett, R.G. Hogan, Geoffrey Hurford, Dave Johnson, Marie Knotts, Mrs V.M. Leather, Audrey Leonard, Carole Lucas, Josephine Mutter, Peter Parrish, Ken Phillips, Les Pinner, Edna Pittman, John Pothecary, Sheila Richards, Peter Saunders, Bob Slade, Dorothy Stefano, Doris M. Tryhorn, Edna M. Tryhorn, Beryl Wainwright and Mrs P. Wingrave.

I would also like to express my gratitude to Andrew Holder and Liam McKenna for helping me out on numerous occasions during my transition from using a very old computer to the pleasures of processing words on a modern multi-media PC.

Stock List

(Titles are listed according to the pre-1974 county boundaries)

BERKSHIRE

Wantage
Irene Hancock
ISBN 0-7524-0146 7

CARDIGANSHIRE

Aberaeron and Mid Ceredigion
William Howells
ISBN 0-7524-0106-8

CHESHIRE

Ashton-under-Lyne and Mossley
Alice Lock
ISBN 0-7524-0164-5

Around Bebington
Pat O'Brien
ISBN 0-7524-0121-1

Crewe
Brian Edge
ISBN 0-7524-0052-5

Frodsham and Helsby
Frodsham and District Local History Group
ISBN 0-7524-0161-0

Macclesfield Silk
Moira Stevenson and Louanne Collins
ISBN 0-7524-0315 X

Marple
Steve Cliffe
ISBN 0-7524-0316-8

Runcorn
Bert Starkey
ISBN 0-7524-0025-8

Warrington
Janice Hayes
ISBN 0-7524-0040-1

West Kirby to Hoylake
Jim O'Neil
ISBN 0-7524-0024-X

Widnes
Anne Hall and the Widnes Historical Society
ISBN 0-7524-0117-3

CORNWALL

Padstow
Malcolm McCarthy
ISBN 0-7524-0033-9

St Ives Bay
Jonathan Holmes
ISBN 0-7524-0186-6

COUNTY DURHAM

Bishop Auckland
John Land
ISBN 0-7524-0312-5

Around Shildon
Vera Chapman
ISBN 0-7524-0115-7

CUMBERLAND

Carlisle
Dennis Perriam
ISBN 0-7524-0166-1

DERBYSHIRE

Around Alfreton
Alfreton and District Heritage Trust
ISBN 0-7524-0041-X

Barlborough, Clowne, Creswell and Whitwell
Les Yaw
ISBN 0-7524-0031-2

Around Bolsover
Bernard Haigh
ISBN 0-7524-0021-5

Around Derby
Alan Champion and Mark Edworthy
ISBN 0-7524-0020-7

Long Eaton
John Barker
ISBN 0-7524-0110-6

Ripley and Codnor
David Buxton
ISBN 0-7524-0042-8

Shirebrook
Geoff Sadler
ISBN 0-7524-0028-2

Shirebrook: A Second Selection
Geoff Sadler
ISBN 0-7524-0317-6

DEVON

Brixham
Ted Gosling and Lyn Marshall
ISBN 0-7524-0037-1

Around Honiton
Les Berry and Gerald Gosling
ISBN 0-7524-0175-0

Around Newton Abbot
Les Berry and Gerald Gosling
ISBN 0-7524-0027-4

Around Ottery St Mary
Gerald Gosling and Peter Harris
ISBN 0-7524-0030-4

Around Sidmouth
Les Berry and Gerald Gosling
ISBN 0-7524-0137-8

DORSET

Around Uplyme and Lyme Regis
Les Berry and Gerald Gosling
ISBN 0-7524-0044-4

ESSEX

Braintree and Bocking
John and Sandra Adlam and Mark Charlton
ISBN 0-7524-0129-7

Ilford
Ian Dowling and Nick Harris
ISBN 0-7524-0050-9

Ilford: A Second Selection
Ian Dowling and Nick Harris
ISBN 0-7524-0320-6

Saffron Walden
Jean Gumbrell
ISBN 0-7524-0176-9

GLAMORGAN

Around Bridgend
Simon Eckley
ISBN 0-7524-0189-0

Caerphilly
Simon Eckley
ISBN 0-7524-0194-7

Around Kenfig Hill and Pyle
Keith Morgan
ISBN 0-7524-0314-1

The County Borough of Merthyr Tydfil
Carolyn Jacob, Stephen Done and Simon Eckley
ISBN 0-7524-0012-6

Mountain Ash, Penrhiwceiber and Abercynon
Bernard Baldwin and Harry Rogers
ISBN 0-7524-0114-9

Pontypridd
Simon Eckley
ISBN 0-7524-0017-7

Rhondda
Simon Eckley and Emrys Jenkins
ISBN 0-7524-0028-2

Rhondda: A Second Selection
Simon Eckley and Emrys Jenkins
ISBN 0-7524-0308-7

Roath, Splott, and Adamsdown
Roath Local History Society
ISBN 0-7524-0199-8

GLOUCESTERSHIRE

Barnwood, Hucclecote and Brockworth
Alan Sutton
ISBN 0-7524-0000-2

Forest to Severn
Humphrey Phelps
ISBN 0-7524-0008-8

Filton and the Flying Machine
Malcolm Hall
ISBN 0-7524-0171-8

Gloster Aircraft Company
Derek James
ISBN 0-7524-0038-X

The City of Gloucester
Jill Voyce
ISBN 0-7524-0306-0

Around Nailsworth and Minchinhampton from the Conway Collection
Howard Beard
ISBN 0-7524-0048-7

Around Newent
Tim Ward
ISBN 0-7524-0003-7

Stroud: Five Stroud Photographers
Howard Beard, Peter Harris and Wilf Merrett
ISBN 0-7524-0305-2

HAMPSHIRE

Gosport
Ian Edelman
ISBN 0-7524-0300-1

Winchester from the Sollars Collection
John Brimfield
ISBN 0-7524-0173-4

HEREFORDSHIRE
Ross-on-Wye
Tom Rigby and Alan Sutton
ISBN 0-7524-0002-9

HERTFORDSHIRE
Buntingford
Philip Plumb
ISBN 0-7524-0170-X

Hampstead Garden Suburb
Mervyn Miller
ISBN 0-7524-0319-2

Hemel Hempstead
Eve Davis
ISBN 0-7524-0167-X

Letchworth
Mervyn Miller
ISBN 0-7524-0318-4

Welwyn Garden City
Angela Eserin
ISBN 0-7524-0133-5

KENT
Hythe
Joy Melville and Angela Lewis-Johnson
ISBN 0-7524-0169-6

North Thanet Coast
Alan Kay
ISBN 0-7524-0112-2

Shorts Aircraft
Mike Hooks
ISBN 0-7524-0193-9

LANCASHIRE
Lancaster and the Lune Valley
Robert Alston
ISBN 0-7524-0015-0

Morecambe Bay
Robert Alston
ISBN 0-7524-0163-7

Manchester
Peter Stewart
ISBN 0-7524-0103-3

LINCOLNSHIRE
Louth
David Cuppleditch
ISBN 0-7524-0172-6

Stamford
David Gerard
ISBN 0-7524-0309-5

LONDON
(Greater London and Middlesex)

Battersea and Clapham
Patrick Loobey
ISBN 0-7524-0010-X

Canning Town
Howard Bloch and Nick Harris
ISBN 0-7524-0057-6

Chiswick
Carolyn and Peter Hammond
ISBN 0-7524-0001-0

Forest Gate
Nick Harris and Dorcas Sanders
ISBN 0-7524-0049-5

Greenwich
Barbara Ludlow
ISBN 0-7524-0045-2

Highgate and Muswell Hill
Joan Schwitzer and Ken Gay
ISBN 0-7524-0119-X

Islington
Gavin Smith
ISBN 0-7524-0140-8

Lewisham
John Coulter and Barry Olley
ISBN 0-7524-0059-2

Leyton and Leytonstone
Keith Romig and Peter Lawrence
ISBN 0-7524-0158-0

Newham Dockland
Howard Bloch
ISBN 0-7524-0107-6

Norwood
Nicholas Reed
ISBN 0-7524-0147-5

Peckham and Nunhead
John D. Beasley
ISBN 0-7524-0122-X

Piccadilly Circus
David Oxford
ISBN 0-7524-0196-3

Stoke Newington
Gavin Smith
ISBN 0-7524-0159-9

Sydenham and Forest Hill
John Coulter and John Seaman
ISBN 0-7524-0036-3

Wandsworth
Patrick Loobey
ISBN 0-7524-0026-6

Wanstead and Woodford
Ian Dowling and Nick Harris
ISBN 0-7524-0113-0

MONMOUTHSHIRE

Vanished Abergavenny
Frank Olding
ISBN 0-7524-0034-7

Abertillery, Aberbeeg and Llanhilleth
Abertillery and District Museum Society and Simon Eckley
ISBN 0-7524-0134-3

Blaina, Nantyglo and Brynmawr
Trevor Rowson
ISBN 0-7524-0136-X

NORFOLK

North Norfolk
Cliff Richard Temple
ISBN 0-7524-0149-1

NOTTINGHAMSHIRE

Nottingham 1897–1947
Douglas Whitworth
ISBN 0-7524-0157-2

OXFORDSHIRE

Banbury
Tom Rigby
ISBN 0-7524-0013-4

PEMBROKESHIRE

Saundersfoot and Tenby
Ken Daniels
ISBN 0-7524-0192-0

RADNORSHIRE

Llandrindod Wells
Chris Wilson
ISBN 0-7524-0191-2

SHROPSHIRE

Leominster
Eric Turton
ISBN 0-7524-0307-9

Ludlow
David Lloyd
ISBN 0-7524-0155-6

Oswestry
Bernard Mitchell
ISBN 0-7524-0032-0

North Telford: Wellington, Oakengates, and Surrounding Areas
John Powell and Michael A. Vanns
ISBN 0-7524-0124-6

South Telford: Ironbridge Gorge, Madeley, and Dawley
John Powell and Michael A. Vanns
ISBN 0-7524-0125-4

SOMERSET

Bath
Paul De'Ath
ISBN 0-7524-0127-0

Around Yeovil
Robin Ansell and Marion Barnes
ISBN 0-7524-0178-5

STAFFORDSHIRE

Cannock Chase
Sherry Belcher and Mary Mills
ISBN 0-7524-0051-7

Around Cheadle
George Short
ISBN 0-7524-0022-3

The Potteries
Ian Lawley
ISBN 0-7524-0046-0

East Staffordshire
Geoffrey Sowerby and Richard Farman
ISBN 0-7524-0197-1

SUFFOLK

Lowestoft to Southwold
Humphrey Phelps
ISBN 0-7524-0108-4

Walberswick to Felixstowe
Humphrey Phelps
ISBN 0-7524-0109-2

SURREY

Around Camberley
Ken Clarke
ISBN 0-7524-0148-3

Around Cranleigh
Michael Miller
ISBN 0-7524-0143-2

Epsom and Ewell
Richard Essen
ISBN 0-7524-0111-4

Farnham by the Wey
Jean Parratt
ISBN 0-7524-0185-8

Industrious Surrey: Historic Images of the County at Work
Chris Shepheard
ISBN 0-7524-0009-6

Reigate and Redhill
Mary G. Goss
ISBN 0-7524-0179-3

Richmond and Kew
Richard Essen
ISBN 0-7524-0145-9

SUSSEX

Billingshurst
Wendy Lines
ISBN 0-7524-0301-X

WARWICKSHIRE

Central Birmingham 1870–1920
Keith Turner
ISBN 0-7524-0053-3

Old Harborne
Roy Clarke
ISBN 0-7524-0054-1

WILTSHIRE

Malmesbury
Dorothy Barnes
ISBN 0-7524-0177-7

Great Western Swindon
Tim Bryan
ISBN 0-7524-0153-X

Midland and South Western Junction Railway
Mike Barnsley and Brian Bridgeman
ISBN 0-7524-0016-9

WORCESTERSHIRE

Around Malvern
Keith Smith
ISBN 0-7524-0029-0

YORKSHIRE
(EAST RIDING)

Hornsea
G.L. Southwell
ISBN 0-7524-0120-3

YORKSHIRE
(NORTH RIDING)

Northallerton
Vera Chapman
ISBN 0-7524-055-X

Scarborough in the 1970s and 1980s
Richard Percy
ISBN 0-7524-0325-7

YORKSHIRE
(WEST RIDING)

Barnsley
Barnsley Archive Service
ISBN 0-7524-0188-2

Bingley
Bingley and District Local History Society
ISBN 0-7524-0311-7

Bradford
Gary Firth
ISBN 0-7524-0313-3

Castleford
Wakefield Metropolitan District Council
ISBN 0-7524-0047-9

Doncaster
Peter Tuffrey
ISBN 0-7524-0162-9

Harrogate
Malcolm Neesam
ISBN 0-7524-0154-8

Holme Valley
Peter and Iris Bullock
ISBN 0-7524-0139-4

Horsforth
Alan Cockroft and Matthew Young
ISBN 0-7524-0130-0

Knaresborough
Arnold Kellett
ISBN 0-7524-0131-9

Around Leeds
Matthew Young and Dorothy Payne
ISBN 0-7524-0168-8

Penistone
Matthew Young and David Hambleton
ISBN 0-7524-0138-6

Selby from the William Rawling Collection
Matthew Young
ISBN 0-7524-0198-X

Central Sheffield
Martin Olive
ISBN 0-7524-0011-8

Around Stocksbridge
Stocksbridge and District History Society
ISBN 0-7524-0165-3

TRANSPORT

Filton and the Flying Machine
Malcolm Hall
ISBN 0-7524-0171-8

Gloster Aircraft Company
Derek James
ISBN 0-7524-0038-X

Great Western Swindon
Tim Bryan
ISBN 0-7524-0153-X

Midland and South Western Junction Railway
Mike Barnsley and Brian Bridgeman
ISBN 0-7524-0016-9

Shorts Aircraft
Mike Hooks
ISBN 0-7524-0193-9

This stock list shows all titles available in the United Kingdom as at 30 September 1995.

ORDER FORM

The books in this stock list are available from your local bookshop. Alternatively they are available by mail order at a totally inclusive price of £10.00 per copy.

For overseas orders please add the following postage supplement for each copy ordered:
> European Union £0.36 (this includes the Republic of Ireland)
> Royal Mail Zone 1 (for example, U.S.A. and Canada) £1.96
> Royal Mail Zone 2 (for example, Australia and New Zealand) £2.47

Please note that all of these supplements are actual Royal Mail charges with no profit element to the Chalford Publishing Company. Furthermore, as the Air Mail Printed Papers rate applies, we are restricted from enclosing any personal correspondence other than to indicate the senders name.

Payment can be made by cheque, Visa or Mastercard. Please indicate your method of payment on this order form.

If you are not entirely happy with your purchase you may return it within 30 days of receipt for a full refund.

Please send your order to:

> The Chalford Publishing Company,
> St Mary's Mill,
> Chalford,
> Stroud,
> Gloucestershire
> GL6 8NX

This order form should perforate away from the book. However, if you are reluctant to damage the book in any way we are quite happy to accept a photocopy order form or a letter containing the necessary information.

PLEASE WRITE CLEARLY USING BLOCK CAPITALS

Name and address of the person ordering the books listed below:

_____

_____

_____ Post code _____

Please also supply your telephone number in case we have difficulty fully understanding your requirements.　　Tel.: _____ - _____

Name and address of where the books are to be despatched to (if different from above):

_____

_____

_____ Post code _____

Please indicate here if you would like to receive future information on books published by the Chalford Publishing Company.

___ Yes, please put me on your mailing list　　___ No, please just send the books ordered below

Title	ISBN	Quantity
....	0-7524-_____-___	_____
....	0-7524-_____-___	_____
....	0-7524-_____-___	_____
....	0-7524-_____-___	_____
....	0-7524-_____-___	_____
	Total number of books	_____

Cost of books delivered in UK = Number of books ordered @ £10 each =£ _____

Overseas postage supplement (if relevant)　　　　　　　　=£ _____

TOTAL PAYMENT　　　　　　　　　　　　　　　　=£ _____

Method of Payment　　　❑ Cheque　　❑ Visa　　❑ Mastercard　　**VISA**

Please make cheques payable to *The Chalford Publishing Company*　　MasterCard

Name of Card Holder　　_____

Card Number　❏❏❏❏❏❏❏❏❏❏❏❏❏❏❏❏❏❏❏❏

Expiry date　❏❏ / ❏❏

I authorise payment of £_____ from the above card

Signed _____